Childhood Experiences Influence Women's Mental Well-being

Mary T. Morgan

ABSTRACT

Early identification of adverse childhood experiences can help children get traumainformed care earlier in life before lifelong psychological or physical damage can result. This research project was an investigation into the relationship between the adverse childhood experiences of sexual abuse and substance use disorder, along with the independent variables of age, sex, income, education level, marital status, and employment among women with a history of domestic violence. Bronfenbrenner's social ecological model served as the theoretical framework. Archival data from the Behavior Risk Factor Surveillance Study for South Carolina from 2020 to 2021 were used for analyses. As education level increased, days of poor mental health decreased ($OR = .700$, 95% CI .600-.817). As marital status changed from married ($OR = .501$, 95% CI .322- .755) to divorced ($OR = .657$, 95% CI .106-.406), there remained a decrease in days of poor mental health. As income increased, days of poor mental health decreased ($OR = .781$, 95% CI .691-.884). Sexual abuse by being made to touch someone once ($OR = 9.54$, 95% CI 1.17-77.64) was associated with an increase in mental health days not good. Continuing work with local and state entities to identify additional opportunities to identify ACEs at pivotal contact points is an important first step. Early identification of ACEs in girls below age 18 will lead to trauma-informed care to mitigate psychological or physical harm to help improve positive mental health outcomes and social change in adulthood.

Contents

Chapter 1: Introduction to the Study Introduction to the Study

Introduction

According to the Centers for Disease Control and Prevention (CDC) and the

National Center for Injury Prevention and Control (NCIPC, 2022), South

Carolina ranks 12th for domestic violence against women. Updated statistics

for 2023 showed that 41.5% of women in South Carolina experience some

form of domestic violence, such as those previously identified (Domestic

Violence by State 2023, n.d.). The national average is 41% (Domestic

Violence by State 2023, n.d.). An adverse childhood experience (ACE) is a

trauma experienced during childhood before age 18 (CDC et al., 2021; Felitti,

2019).

There are 10 ACEs in three categories: (a) *Child Mistreatment*

(physical, sexual, or emotional mistreatment), (b) *Neglect* (emotional and

physical), and (c) *Household Dysfunction* (emotional malfunction, parent

absenteeism due to incarceration, separation/divorce, substance use disorder,

and physical violence against the mother) (Loxton et al., 2020; Ports et al.,

2022). Witnessing one instance of an ACE or living through chronic ACEs

exposures during childhood has been documented to cause trauma affecting

the developing brain, disruption of cognitive development, leads to adverse

health outcomes in adulthood, and maladaptive social functioning (Fisher,

2019; Loxton et al., 2021; Ports et al., 2022).

I investigated the relationship between sexual abuse and household

substance use disorder and their individual and combined influences on the mental health of women with a history of domestic violence. Further supporting the research, the background and problem statement will provide a basis for the study rationale. Reviewing the theoretical

framework will provide a foundation for public health policy development. Combined with the literature review, methodology, analysis, and final discussion of the outcome, it will provide a well-rounded investigative discussion of the issue and possible mitigative efforts.

Background

Researchers have demonstrated worsening adult outcomes from ACEs exposure statistics based on demographic factors (Jones et al., 2021a; Loxton et al., 2021; Ports et al., 2022). For some groups, the risk increases due to social and cultural factors (Jones et al., 2021a; Loxton et al., 2021; Ports et al., 2022). Additionally, research supports findings that belonging to a particular minority group may increase the risk due to societal challenges such as socioeconomic inequalities, environmental differences, health challenges, and household instability (Ports et al., 2022). According to Bryngeirsdottir et al. (2022), some women are denied even the most basic of opportunities, such as work, education, or a lack of control over their bodies. Felitti (2019) led the way for ACEs research to become mainstream, such that it is now included in annual health status surveys conducted by the CDC.

Based on this initial research, there are now others in public health studying how ACEs impact chronic emotional and physical health conditions and what public health policies can be amended and developed to reduce and even prevent them (Boppre et al., 2021; Decker et al., 2019; Jasthi et al., 2022; Ports et al., 2022). Currently, researchers have focused more on domestic violence, sexual abuse, and household substance use disorder as independent or cumulative contributors to maladaptive behaviors, chronic health conditions, and challenging outcomes related to emotional illness (Boppre et al., 2021; Jasthi et al., 2022; Ports et al., 2022; Sheffler et al., 2022). However, few studies investigated how sexual abuse and substance use disorder and the mental health of women with a history of domestic violence are related (Jasthi et al., 2022; Pace et al., 2022; Pokharel et al., 2020).

There is research available on ACEs influence on mental health and the victimization of adolescents that leads to adverse outcomes in adulthood regarding overall functioning (Westermair et al., 2018). It is estimated that during their lifetime, approximately 36% or one-third of women in the United States will experience sexual or physical aggression (Decker et al., 2019; Jones et al., 2018). Others indicate that millions of adult men and women fall victim to domestic violence (Nikulina et al., 2021). Another 21% of women have been victims of rape or other sexual violence (Decker et al., 2019). Furthermore, from research, we understand that victims of domestic violence remain at increased risk for adverse life outcomes in areas such as mental health, self-care, substance misuse, and difficulty with academic progression and completion. Nikulina et al. (2021) have suggested that prevalence rates for domestic violence are between 12% and 72%, and approximately half of all domestic violence victims report experiencing their first victimization in their emerging adult years (Nikulina et al., 2021). Decker et al. (2019) indicate that roughly 22% of women experience domestic violence during the emerging adult years of ages 11 – 17.

Furthermore, they suggest that the highest prevalence rates for domestic violence is found in Black women at 44%, American Indians and Alaskan Natives at 46%, and Multiracial at 54%. White women represented the lowest domestic violence prevalence of 35% (Decker et al., 2019). Forty-three percent of women, compared to only 8% of men, experience multiple forms of domestic violence. In comparison, "current or former intimate partners" are responsible for more than half of homicidal crimes against women compared to roughly 8% against men (Decker et al., 2019). The literature supports the fact that women experience more physical and sexual acts of aggression and assault. The current literature review also strengthens the reason for further study of the female population regarding investigating an improved understanding of how ACEs adversely affect adult functioning. This study is designed to investigate the relationship between sexual abuse and substance use disorder and the mental health of women with a history of domestic violence.

Researchers considered resiliency factors that helped women survive chronic forms of domestic violence (Bryngeirsdottir et al., 2022; Decker et al., 2019). Depression, PTSD, anxiety, and bipolar disorder (BPD) are some

of the most identified diagnoses in women who come from an environment of

household dysfunction (Jones et al., 2018). Further investigative research is

necessary to mitigate the situations that contribute to the resulting physical

and mental difficulties.

This study is needed to help evolve the provision of services to women

with a history of domestic violence. The State of South Carolina started

participating in the

ACEs component of the annual Behavior Risk Factor Surveillance Survey

(BRFSS) in 2009 (CDC et al., 2022). The BRFSS was developed to provide

state level data on health behaviors that were being monitored on a national

basis by the National Center for Health Statistics since the 1980s (NCCDP et

al., 2014). The survey was first employed in 1993 to reduce poor

consequences from behavior choices (NCCDP et al., 2014). However, to

monitor and develop plans to reduce the declining health and behavioral

risks, a method had to be developed to track and support goal development

and accomplishment statewide (NCCDP et al., 2014).

The BRFSS was devised as a telephonic survey to gather information

on behaviors related to chronic diseases that may lead to premature death and

comorbidities (NCCDP et al., 2014). Because it is employed via telephone, it

is cost-effective and can reach those in very remote areas (NCCDP et al.,

2014). After testing using initial surveys in 29 states between 1981 and 1983, the first BRFSS questionnaire was used in 1984, with 15 states where monthly data collection was completed (NCCDP et al., 2014). This led to the development of core questions that gathered information on health behaviors such as smoking, substance use, physical activity, nutrition, heart disease, and automobile safety around seat belt use (NCCDP et al., 2014). In 1988, the CDC added the optional modules, and the BRFSS became a national standard way of surveying health-related behavior in 1988 (NCCDP et al., 2014).

The CDC began using the ACEs questionnaire in 1998 (Felitti, 2019; Ports et al., 2022). Based on the ACEs surveys, evidence is beginning to demonstrate the need for trauma-focused intervention at the school-age level (Felitti, 2019; Ports et al., 2022).
With continued statewide participation in the ACEs component of the BRFSS, South Carolina will continue to assess the status of childhood trauma. This will lead to the necessity of appropriate mitigation to address disclosed traumas.

The results of this study can be used to explain to community leaders the importance of the potentially damaging effects of individual and chronic ACEs exposure during the formative years of childhood development. With this understanding, appropriate assessment can be completed by pediatric care professionals and professionals providing services to women of domestic violence. Incorporating

Bronfenbrenner's social ecological model, the connection to environmental factors is also considered (Bronfenbrenner, 1979). Factors such as age, sex, marital status, employment status, income level, and education may also influence the mental health of women with a history of domestic violence (Bronfenbrenner, 1979; Jasthi et al., 2022). Grounding this research in the theory of Bronfenbrenner's social ecological model, the results will be shared at the microsystem, mesosystem, and macrosystem levels (Bronfenbrenner, 1979). Through thorough assessment, planning, and policy development, ACEs influences can be better understood, and appropriate intervention measures can be planned for.

Problem Statement

The research problem addressed in this study is the lack of early identification of childhood traumas, or ACEs. Early identification of ACEs provides an opportunity to implement strategies for appropriate intervention, develop meaningful public health policies to decrease the frequency of ACEs occurrences, promote healthy outcomes in adulthood, and educate the community on the importance of identifying and preventing

ACEs (McLennan et al., 2022). Childhood trauma permeates society. When unidentified or ignored, it shows up at the worst time (Nikulina et al., 2021). As an adult, it manifests in an inability to distinguish positive or negative relationships resulting from emotional or physical abuse witnessed during childhood (Nikulina et al., 2021). It may show up as a chronic health condition due to prolonged periods of hypervigilance (Fisher, 2019).

Individuals may have witnessed these behaviors through reports from the media (Fisher, 2019). For example, when coworkers who physically retaliate against others in the workplace exhibit maladaptive behavior, they may have learned this as young children or in adolescence (Fisher, 2019). Or those who abuse alcohol or drugs as a manner of self-medicating difficulties in life (Fisher, 2019). In some instances, adult behavior and responses to trauma can be a direct result of a lack of intervention to manage the past trauma (Fisher, 2019).

More than 2 decades ago, Felitti (2019) conducted the initial ACEs study with Kaiser Permanente and the CDC. This initial study examined how childhood trauma influenced adult behavior and health outcomes (Felitti, 2019). Following participants throughout their lifespan, they documented chronic health conditions such as obesity, stress, or other mental health conditions, including substance use (Felitti, 2019). In Felitti's work with obese patients, it became apparent that although the patients were successfully losing weight, they hit a plateau and began gaining back the lost weight. Felitti questioned the reason for the reversal and discovered that the patients were dealing with childhood traumas as adults. Felitti applied the ACEs questionnaire in his patient encounters. Patients declined to participate as they did not like the retrospective review of childhood memories and began to drop out of the study. Hospitals began to decline the inclusion of the ACEs questionnaire with their patients due to the concerns they voiced

(Felitti, 2019).

Recently, public health professionals have understood that ACEs are integral to adult development (Dube, 2022). Research continues to inform knowledge, public health practice, and policies to begin to disrupt cycles of perpetual childhood trauma and its suffocating grip on adulthood (Dube, 2022). ACEs have been examined regarding their cumulative and individual influences on health (Merrick et al., 2019), mental health (Pace et al., 2022; Westermair et al., 2018; Willie et al., 2021; Witt et al., 2019), pregnant women (Jasthi et al., 2022), and other adulthood characteristics for men and women

(Decker et al., Jones et al., 2018; Jones et al., 2021a; Jones et al., 2021b; Witt et al. 2019). This project will enhance the written knowledge, enlightening public health practitioners and those interested in reducing the prevalence of the ACEs influences of sexual abuse and substance use disorder on the emotional illness of women with a history of domestic violence.

Purpose of the Study

The purpose of this quantitative predictive study was to investigate how the mental health of women with a history of domestic violence is impacted by sexual abuse and substance use disorder.

Nature of the Study

The aim of this study was to investigate age, sex, marital status, income, education, employment status, sexual abuse, and substance use disorder and their relationship to the mental health of women with a history of domestic violence. The dependent variable is mental health. The independent variables are age, sex, marital status, income level, education, employment status, sex abuse, and substance use disorder. Although the population is defined as women with a history of domestic violence, domestic violence will be treated as an independent variable. The participants selected for the study were females responding to a history of domestic violence or mental health on the 2021 BRFSS.

This study will help inform providers of services to children ages 18 and below of the importance of including ACEs assessments in their intake and screening procedures.

This will help identify ACEs exposure so that the appropriate intervention can be offered. This study may help inform policy development so that future initiatives include services targeting children, and the positive effects may benefit them in adulthood. As adults, they would have developed coping skills to assist them in making more informed life decisions, which should lead to decreased chronic and mental health and risky behavior participation.

Research Questions

RQ1: What is the relationship between mental health and age, sex, and education of women with or without a history of domestic violence?

H_{10}: There will be no relationship between mental health and age, sex, and education of women with or without a history of domestic violence.

H_{1a}: There will be a relationship between mental health and age, sex, and education of women with or without a history of domestic violence.

RQ2: What is the relationship between mental health and marital status, income level, and employment in women with or without a history of domestic violence?

H_{20}: There will be no relationship between mental health and marital status, income level, and employment in women with or without a history of domestic violence.

H_{2a}: There will be a relationship between mental health and marital status, income level, and employment in women with or without a history of domestic violence. RQ3: What is the relationship between mental health and sexual abuse, and substance use disorder in women with and without a history of domestic violence? H_{30}: There will be no relationship between mental health and sexual abuse and substance use disorder in women with or without a history of domestic violence. H_{3a}: There will be a

relationship between mental health and sexual abuse and substance use
disorder in women with or without a history of domestic violence.

Definitions

Age: It is defined as the respondent age 18 or older (CDC et al., pp. 11& 15,
2021).

Domestic violence: It is defined as the frequency a parent or adult in
the home, when the respondent was under 18, hit, beat, kick, or cause
physical hurt in any way (CDC et al., p. 110, 2021).

Education level: It is defined as never attended school or only kindergarten,
Grades 1 through 8 (elementary), Grades 9 through 11 (some high school),
Grade 12 or GED (high school graduate), college 1 year to 3 years (some
college or technical school), college four years or more (college graduate),
and refused (CDC et al., p. 37, 2021) *Employment status:* It is defined as
employed for wages, self-employed, out of work for one year or more, out of
work for more than one year, a homemaker, a student, retired, unable to
work, and refused (CDC et al., p. 40, 2021).

Income: It is defined as less than $10,000 incrementally to more than
$200,000. It is also defined as don't know or not sure and refused (CDC et
al., p. 41, 2021).

Marital status: It is defined as married, divorced, widowed, separated,
never married, or a member of an unmarried couple (CDC et al., p. 38, 2021).

Mental health: It is defined as problems with stress, depression, or emotions within the past 30 days of the response being collected (CDC et al., p. 20, 2021). Mental health is also defined as the number of days in the past 30 days the respondent experienced poor physical or mental health that kept them from doing their usual activities, such as self-care, work, or recreation (CDC et al., p. 21, 2021). It is also defined as ever being told by a doctor, nurse, or another health professional that one had a depressive disorder (including depression, major depression, dysthymia, or minor depression;) (CDC et al., pp. 20-21, 2021). Mental health is combined with physical health to review conditions for the past 30 days that prevented the respondent from doing regular activities, self-care, work, or recreation (CDC et al., pp. 20-21, 2021).

Sex: It is defined as male or female (CDC et al., pp. 11-12, 2021).

Sexual abuse: It is defined as the frequency of being touched sexually by someone at least five years older than the respondent or an adult (CDC et al., pp. 111112, 2021). It is also defined as the number of times that anyone at least five years older than the respondent or an adult tried to make the respondent touch them sexually (CDC et al., pp. 111-112, 2021). It is also defined as the frequency that anyone at least 5 years or older than the respondent tried to force the respondent to have sex (CDC et al., pp. 111112, 2021).

Substance use disorder: It is defined as the individual living with anyone who was a problem drinker or alcoholic, who abused prescription medications, or used illegal street drugs (CDC et al., pp. 107-108, 2021).

Contextual Assumptions

It is assumed that an increase in the number of times the ACE is experienced or the accumulation of ACEs is related to an increase in adverse outcomes in adulthood (Dube, 2022; Felitti, 2019; Ports et al., 2022). It is also an assumption that there must be a generational approach to providing trauma-informed care (TIC) for those who have experienced a variety of ACEs involvement (Dube, 2022). These assumptions are necessary for this study because this is the anticipated and validated research outcome thus far from the literature (Dube, 2022; Felitti, 2019; Ports et al., 2022). Parents who were themselves exposed to ACEs and now have children must understand that their past does not have to be repeated on their children. Technology and research have allowed them to learn from past experiences and rise above those challenging circumstances to a brighter and better future.

By investigating the relationship between mental health in women with a history of domestic violence and the independent variables and identified ACEs, the relationships between more than two independent variables (sexual abuse, substance use disorder, domestic violence, age, sex, education, income level, marital status, employment) and one dependent variable (mental health) will ideally be identified. Because the

dependent variable is ordinal, multivariate ordinal logistic regression will

allow for the investigation of statistically significant effects of the

independent variables on the dependent variable

(Laerd Statistics, n.d.).

Scope and Delimitations

The population of interest for this study is women over the age of 18

with a history of domestic violence. Excluded from the study are men and

women with chronic health conditions. Theoretical frameworks of

consideration to help prevent future instances of ACEs occurring are key to

the success of any policy or program development. The Health Belief Model

(HBM) is a concept built upon the beliefs of the individual in whom the

change is expected (Hayden, 2019). The basic premise is that the individual's

perspective concerning the health problem is affected by various inter and

intra-personal beliefs (Hayden, 2019). Cultural and societal interactions that

temper these beliefs and experiences throughout the lifespan are based upon

perceived threats, opportunities, seriousness, and susceptibility (Hayden,

2019). Lacking are additional societal interactions with the community and

institutions (Hayden, 2019). The Theory of Reasoned Action (TRA) suggests

that each person has a strong will to control participation in a behavior

(Hayden, 2019). Although young children may have a strong will to not obey at times, they do not have volition over adults who threaten them into submission due to a power difference (Hayden, 2019).

Researchers must review the multitude of available theoretical constructs and select the model best suited to the research project, questions, and hypotheses. The researcher should consider the variables, the population, societal and cultural influences, and the potential personal contributing factors for the population of interest (Hayden, 2019). Given that the population of interest is in South Carolina, the study outcomes should be generalizable to other states as the data is drawn from a national survey, and the ACEs questions are standard across all states that elect to have them included in their surveys. This research study should be generalizable if conducted in any other state with

ACEs modules included.

Bronfenbrenner's (1979) social ecological model was the most appropriate theoretical framework for this research project. I investigated the relationship between the frequency of occurrences of sexual abuse along with substance use disorder and mental health. Because I investigated behavior from the view of the individual post trauma, it was important to consider the independent variables' influence on the individual's personal and societal interactions. The independent variables of age, sex, and marital status were represented in the microsystem or personal environment (Bronfenbrenner, 1979; Hayden, 2019). The independent variables of income, education, and employment were identified at the macrosystem or community level

(Bronfenbrenner, 1979; Hayden, 2019). Sexual abuse and substance use

disorder are associated with the exosystem or institutional environment as

one seeks assistance addressing those concerns

(Bronfenbrenner, 1979; Hayden, 2019).

This theory can be used to investigate childhood development through

age 18 as one grows and evolves through various levels of the model and how

each level contributes to the emerging adult (Bronfenbrenner, 1979; Hayden,

2019). It can be used to understand the individual's personality traits, beliefs,

and cultural aspects of decisionmaking as an adult (Hayden, 2019).

Bronfenbrenner (1979) suggested that the social ecological model comprises

multiple levels that people will interact with throughout their lifespan.

Meeting the individual where they are as an adult while considering their

upbringing will provide a more holistic opportunity to meet their needs.

To thoroughly investigate this public health dilemma, human behavior

combined with the prediction tools of statistical analysis on future behavior

were considered (Gerstman, 2015; Hayden, 2019). The social ecological

model was the most appropriate theoretical framework to apply in the holistic

investigation demonstrating the significance of a relationship between sexual

abuse, substance use disorder, age, sex, education, marital status, income

level, and employment to the mental health of women with a history of

domestic violence (Abbas & Jabeen, 2023; Hayden, 2019). Combining behavioral and mathematical science allowed for reviewing and revising current and future public health policy.

Limitations

The ACEs questionnaire was limited regarding the optional questions that could be included or excluded. Some professionals have requested that the ACEs definitions be revised and expanded to include other traumas the original questionnaire did not capture. This would profoundly affect the validity, reliability, and sensitivity of the current tool

(Afifi, 2022). The theoretical construct for policy development was Bronfenbrenner's social ecological model. Other researchers may have preferred other theories based on their revision of the research outcomes. At this time, no known personal biases may affect the study outcomes. As identified above, limitations are mitigated by following the current best practice standards in the field. The BRFSS and ACEs questionnaires, as adopted and utilized by the CDC, were the basis for the variables' definitions, which aligned with the research questions and hypotheses.

Significance

The outcomes from this research will advance knowledge for public health policy development regarding trauma-informed care for children in South Carolina. The outcomes will be shared with those in positions of decision-making capacities so that updated data will increase the knowledge base from which program planning and funding decisions are made. Thereby creating increased capacity for trauma specialists to work with the children

and their parents to begin to enumerate and assist with resources to help

mitigate the ACEs occurrences in homes.

> The ideal result from the outcome data would be that the South
> Carolina

Department of Health and Environmental Control (SCDHEC), the South
Carolina

Department of Mental Health (SCDMH), and the South Carolina Department

of Social Services (SCDSS) would continue unified efforts to address the

ACEs with updated knowledge. For example, current school-based

counselors may be required to have trauma certification to be considered for

an offer of employment. These agencies may consider working unilaterally to

develop complimentary budgets to present to the South Carolina Budget and

Control Board to justify the additional funds to address this issue with better-

trained and equipped staff. Second, through their combined resources, the

state agencies could engage in a communication campaign to address the

ACEs so that they are commonly recognized by any community member, the

affected children, teachers, physicians, friends, and family. Finally, with this

permeation of knowledge of the issue, small steps can start to make a giant

leap forward in years to come. The goal is to help these emerging adults see a

brighter future ahead.

Summary

ACEs currently have devastating impacts on the cognitive
development of adolescents as they transition to adulthood (Felitti, 2019;
Fisher, 2019; Pace et al., 2022; Westermair et al., 2018; Willie et al., 2021;
Witt et al., 2019). Investigating the individual and combined influences of
sexual mistreatment and substance use disorder on emotional illness (Dube,
2022), the plan is to share valuable data that will add to the current body of
knowledge to impact public health policy development for South Carolina to
make a steady, consistent, and lasting change in the lives of children and their
mothers whom ACEs impact. Based on current best practices from the
literature, having statewide, community, and local support, women and
children will learn how to better position themselves for survival and
improved outcomes (Afifi, 2022; Ports et al., 2022; Sheffler et al., 2022;
Stanton et al., 2020).

Chapter 2: Literature Review

Introduction

Early identification of childhood traumas, or ACEs, provides an opportunity to implement strategies for appropriate intervention, develop meaningful public health policies to decrease the frequency of ACEs occurrences, promote healthy outcomes in adulthood, and educate the community on the importance of identifying and preventing ACEs (McLennan et al., 2022). Childhood trauma permeates our society. Unfortunately, when unidentified or ignored, it shows at the worst time (Nikulina et al., 2021). As an adult, it manifests in an inability to distinguish positive or negative relationships resulting from emotional or physical abuse witnessed during childhood (Nikulina et al., 2021). It may show up as a chronic health condition due to prolonged periods of hypervigilance (Fisher, 2019).

Individuals may have witnessed these behaviors through reports from the media (Fisher, 2019). For example, when coworkers who physically retaliate against others in the workplace exhibit maladaptive behavior, they may have learned this as young children or in adolescence (Fisher, 2019). Or those who abuse alcohol or drugs as a manner of self-medicating difficulties in life (Fisher, 2019). In some instances, adult behavior and responses to trauma can be a direct result of a lack of intervention to manage the past trauma (Fisher, 2019).

More than 2 decades ago, Felitti (2019) conducted the initial ACEs study with Kaiser Permanente and the CDC. This initial study examined how childhood trauma influenced adult behavior and health outcomes (Felitti, 2019). Following participants throughout their lifespan, they documented chronic health conditions such as obesity, stress, or other mental health conditions, including substance use (Felitti, 2019). In Felitti's (2020) work with obese patients, it became apparent that although the patients were successfully losing weight, they hit a plateau and began gaining back the lost weight. Felitti (2019) questioned the reason for the reversal and discovered that the patients were dealing with childhood traumas as adults. Felitti (2020) applied the ACEs questionnaire in his patient encounters. Patients declined to participate as they did not like the retrospective review of childhood memories and began to drop out of the study. Hospitals began to decline the inclusion of the ACEs questionnaire with their patients due to the concerns they voiced (Felitti, 2019).

Recently, public health professionals have understood that ACEs are integral to adult development (Dube, 2022). Research continues to inform knowledge, public health practice, and policies to begin to disrupt cycles of perpetual childhood trauma and its suffocating grip on adulthood (Dube, 2022). ACEs have been examined regarding their cumulative and individual influences on health (Merrick et al., 2019), mental health (Pace et al., 2022; Willie et al., 2021; Witt et al., 2019; Westermair et al., 2018), pregnant women (Jasthi et al., 2022), and other adulthood characteristics for men and women (Decker et al., Jones et al., 2018; Jones et al., 2021a; Jones et al., 2021b; Witt et al. 2019). This project will enhance the written knowledge, enlightening public health practitioners and those interested in reducing the prevalence of the ACEs influences of sexual abuse and substance use disorder on the emotional illness of women with a history of domestic violence.

The purpose of this quantitative predictive study is to investigate how the mental health of women with a history of domestic violence is impacted by sexual abuse and substance use disorder. ACEs are traumatic events that occur during childhood between the ages of 0 and 18 years. Some of these events, like physical and sexual abuse, neglect, emotional mistreatment, or dysfunction in the home, have been shown to interfere with the healthy development of young children (Felitti, 2019; Fisher, 2019; Ports et al., 2022). During these years, a child's social, emotional, and physical growth undergoes multiple challenges (Felitti, 2019; Fisher, 2019; Ports et al., 2022). It is normal during these formative years for children to face adversity (Fisher, 2019). However, prolonged, or repeated exposure to such trauma can be detrimental to human development (Fisher, 2019). Elevated body hormones interfere with the brain's functioning, particularly in the amygdala, where the brain constantly scans for fear (Fisher, 2019). The body and the brain begin to live in a constant state of hyperarousal, which is unhealthy over time (Fisher, 2019). Other organs subjected to this increased stress for an extended period may display the stress in chronic health conditions (Fisher, 2019). Another devastating result of sustained exposure to trauma is cognitive impairment (Fisher, 2019; Ports et al., 2022).

Researchers continue to study childhood traumas' influence on adults. Felitti (2019) introduced the inclusion of ACEs more than three decades ago to treat obesity. In the hundreds of patients participating in the obesity program, it became apparent that each patient had a history of sexual or other trauma from childhood that was complicating sustained weight loss success. Felitti worked with the CDC to expand the findings to a larger population (N = 17,337). Based on this in-depth study, Felitti defined ACEs as the categorized experiences of each patient.

Some medical providers have declined to use the ACEs Questionnaire as patients have avoided follow-up visits due to the nature of the questions and not wanting to discuss childhood experiences (Felitti, 2019). The World Health Organization (WHO) implemented the ACEs International Questionnaire (ACE-IQ), which has been employed along with the BRFSS (Felitti, 2019). Other researchers have utilized the ACE-IQ to analyze the prevalence rates of violence, emotional abuse, and bullying in adolescents (Pace et al., 2022). The CDC and Kaiser Permanente also studied ACEs in 1997.

Utilizing a 28-item survey tool, they looked at three key areas, "child abuse

(physical, emotional, sexual abuse), neglect (physical and emotional neglect),

and household challenges (mental illness in the household, substance abuse

in the household, divorce/separation, parental incarceration, and mother

treated violently)" (Ports et al., 2022, p.18).

Nikulina et al. (2021) explained that yearly, more than 10 million

people fall victim to domestic violence. ACEs negatively affect emotional

wellness and overall health functioning in adolescents as they become adults

(Nikulina et al., 2021). I am interested to know what effect, if any, child

mistreatment (sexual abuse) and household dysfunction (substance use

disorder) have on mental health diminution, modulating the cognitive

processes to beneficial decision-making.

Following will be a review of the search parameters to design the

literature review. This will include literature search parameters, the databases

and search engines accessed, the keywords and terms leveraged in the search,

and the span of years. Additionally, an overview of the project's main

premise will follow, including the study supporting the influence of ACEs on

the mental health functioning of women with a history of domestic violence.

The variables will be identified and clarified, along with a review of their

relationship to the theoretical framework.

This literature review is structured to provide the reader with a basic

definition and knowledge of ACEs and how they influence behaviors in adulthood. Most importantly, this literature review is intended to clarify the enigma of mental health and how its' diminution from repeated trauma exposure can adversely affect adult decisionmaking, lifestyle choices, and maladaptive behavioral responses to stress and other life events. All combine to give a liturgical response to exploring how ACEs influence the mental health of women with a history of domestic violence.

Literature Search Strategy

This literature review was conducted utilizing multiple databases such as EBSCOhost, Thoreau, Directory of Open Access Journals, Academic Search Complete,

MEDLINE, Cochrane, ERIC, and Google Scholar, and concluded with Health and Psychosocial. The Thoreau search using *intimate partner violence* AND *women or female* spanned years from 2018 to 2022 and yielded 23,811 results. Accessing the Academic Search Complete database for academic journals with the same search years using *intimate partner violence* AND *aces* OR *adverse childhood experiences* AND *women* OR *female* OR *woman* OR *females* while seeking peer-reviewed articles yielded 131 results. Additional searches were completed using Academic Search Complete, Cochrane Database of Systematic Reviews, ERIC, Health, and Psychosocial Instruments, and MEDLINE with full text with the search terms as indicated above with years limited to 2018 to 2022, full text, and peer-reviewed set as limiters yielded 10,452 results.

The literature search extended to book and articles containing comprehensive research on how ACEs influence the mental health of women with a history of domestic violence. Periodic searches continued from 2018 through 2022 and included any new material that may lend credence to this topic and included keywords such as *intimate partner violence* OR *domestic violence* OR *partner abuse* OR *intimate partner aggression; domestic violence* AND *victims of crime; IPV* AND ACES; *intimate partner violence* AND *aces* AND *women*; IPV, *battered women psychology* AND *substance-related disorders,* AND *domestic violence* AND *women, domestic violence,* AND *women.* Other recent searches included *aces* OR *adverse childhood experiences* OR *childhood trauma* AND *substance use* OR *alcohol and drug abuse* OR *substance abuse* AND *women.*

Some research was more segmented to include studies of the intersectionality of domestic violence, substance use disorder, and emotional illness (St. Cyr et al., 2021). There was also research on incarcerated women with a history of domestic violence regarding the offender and victim perspectives (Day et al., 2018) and even research analyzing the female as the perpetrator of physical violence (Jones et al., 2021). Still, other researchers reviewed the impact of ACEs on the sexual and emotional health of women who had experienced domestic violence (Willie et al., 2021) but failed to provide a data analysis for the frequency and cumulative effects of the ACEs influences of substance misuse and sexual abuse on the mental health of women with a history of domestic violence.

Theoretical Foundation

To adequately address the concerns of ACEs influence on the

emotional wellness of women with a history of domestic violence, there must

be consideration of all environmental, personal, and community interactions

the women may be involved with. In completing the literature review, some

researchers executed studies with women using a feminist theoretical model

(Jones et al., 2018; Jones et al., 2021). Some chose social learning theory

(Nikulina et al., 2021), while some relied upon ecological systems and

cognitive theories (Day et al., 2018). To capture the multiple interactions that

women have with mental health services, physical abuse, and substance use,

Bronfenbrenner's social ecological model is most appropriate (Hayden,

2019).

Bronfenbrenner (1979) suggested that humans adapt and adjust

behaviors based on the frequency of interactions with internal and societal

factors. Multiple forms of indescribable abuse often impact victims, and they

can experience life-changing consequences, making domestic violence a

multi-factorial issue (Bronfenbrenner, 1979; Bryngeirsdottir et al., 2022).

Bronfenbrenner suggested that individuals ebb back and forth between their

intimate environment and external influences during human development. To

have had the greatest effect on an individual, that contact would have had to

be frequent for a significant period (Bronfenbrenner, 1979; Hayden, 2019).

For many victims of domestic violence, emotional mistreatment is perhaps the most consequential. Mental health difficulties are often defined by psychological mistreatment and may include post-traumatic stress disorder or PTSD (Bryngeirsdottir et al., 2022). Applying the hypothesis that the mental health of the abused woman is influenced by trauma, it becomes more apparent how the trauma acts as a barrier to the woman successfully escaping. Bryngeirsdottir et al. (2022) further indicated that posttraumatic growth is a symptom of the mental anguish that occurs long after a victim is free of the abusive relationship. Relationships are formed during childhood and occur along the growth and development of the young child into adulthood (Bronfenbrenner, 1979). It is thought that the final development of an individual is the result of all the formative relationships that have developed along the way and vary based on the individual characteristics of each person (Bronfenbrenner, 1979; Hayden, 2019). Were the social ecological model to be applied to childhood development, the various characteristics of the microsystem, mesosystem, exosystem, macrosystem, and chronosystem would have interacted and intersected at varying points, having a defined effect on the individual's overall development (Bronfenbrenner, 1979; Hayden, 2019). *Note.* Figure 1 represents the social ecological model and corresponding characteristics that support the research questions and hypotheses.

Figure 1

Social Ecological Model

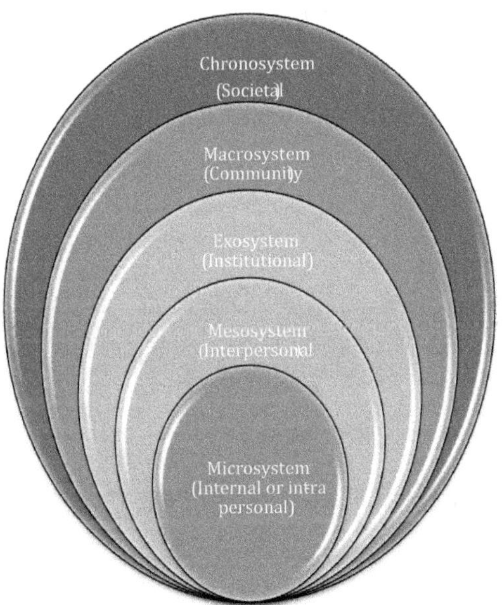

Pokharel et al. (2020) suggested that their analysis revealed multiple

themes at the microsystem level, including but not limited to image perception of the family by external associates, harm to children, a sense of personal responsibility for **domestic violence**, the privacy of managing the **domestic violence**, the shame of the negative perception by others to the abuse, financial concerns, wavering on leaving the relationship, both fear and love for the abuser, hidden negative health impacts, and a lingering sense of loneliness. At this level, one can observe the lack of knowledge described by the participants in the meta-analysis in that there was denial about the abuse accompanied by shame (Pokharel et al., 2020). The participants appeared to be hindered by a lack of health literacy because they were unaware of the resulting chronic health conditions (Pokharel et al., 2020). The belief systems of the participants are observed by the researchers as reported concerns about how friends and family would have interpreted the abuse (Hayden, 2019; Pokharel et al., 2020). This leads to further confusion about leaving the relationship (Hayden, 2019; Pokharel et al., 2020).

This uncertainty is captured in the social ecological model at the mesosystem (interpersonal) level (Bronfenbrenner, 1979; Hayden, 2019). Researchers discussed women's ambivalence over leaving the abusive relationship for many reasons identified at the microsystem (intrapersonal) level (Hayden, 2019; Pokharel et al., 2020). Further explaining that individuals tend to move in and out of these levels interchangeably, relying on their principal beliefs, knowledge, behaviors, attitudes, and personal traits, which influence health literacy and one's ability to make informed choices

(Bronfenbrenner, 1979; Hayden, 2019; Pokharel et al., 2020). Traumatic experiences due to **domestic violence** may have affected the child's development.

At the exosystem (institutional) level, researchers indicated that participants mentioned community partners and health providers not meeting their needs (Pokharel et al., 2020). Hayden (2019) explained that the goal of the exosystem (community) involvement with the individual is to change the environment that encounters the client rather than making the individual conform to the environment. This becomes the most efficacious employment of the health promotion model to positively affect health behavior.

Researchers reported that at the chronosystem (community) level, participants reported being affected by societal norms regarding their views on **domestic violence** and their desired outcomes (Hayden, 2019). The participants reported that society imposed preconceived role expectations for women; thus, disclosing the abuse became cumbersome (Hayden, 2019; Pokharel et al., 2020). Depending on the country and societal expectations, violence against the wife was normalized. With this knowledge, women were reluctant to report violent behavior towards men and even came to accept verbal and emotional abuse as normal behavior (Pokharel et al., 2020). Given this historical perspective of normalized physical violence against women, it makes sense that many remain hesitant to report it or stand up to the perpetrator.

Looking at the framework under consideration, it is possible to see how the individual is nestled in a complicated system of interactions that span the life course, influencing outcomes along the way (Bronfenbrenner, 1979). The woman's decision to remain in an abusive relationship does not begin as an adult (Bronfenbrenner, 1979; Hayden, 2019). It is formed during childhood due to multiple exposures to adverse traumatic events such as substance abuse, physical or sexual aggression in the home, or emotional illness (Nikulina et al., 2021). These events have been studied and are identified as ACEs (Afifi, 2020; Nikulina et al., 2021). Two closely related studies that were similar enough in scope and theoretical perspective were referenced to provide a skeletal structure to emulate (Jones et al., 2018; Nikulina et al., 2021). Having reviewed the theoretical basis for the significance of this study, the key variables will further delineate their importance.

Key Variables

Conceptualization of the Variables

Taillieu et al. (2022) posited that ACEs are segmented into two main categories: childhood mistreatment, "Including physical and sexual abuse, and household dysfunction, including household concerns like parental separation and divorce, mental illness, and substance abuse by adults in the home" (p. 119). Previous studies have provided insight into how physical abuse, sexual abuse, and criminal history impact outcomes for mental health. This research will enhance existing literature on the unique perspective of how sexual abuse and substance use disorder experienced in childhood negatively influence resulting emotional health disorders. Depression, PTSD, anxiety, and bipolar disorder (BPD) are some of the most identified diagnoses in women who come from an environment of household dysfunction (Jones et al., 2018). Other overlooked concerns are criminal offense history and incidences of domestic violence (Jones et al., 2018).

Researchers have demonstrated that increased exposure to ACEs correlates to increased risks of exhibiting exacerbated chronic health conditions, substance misuse, and depressive symptoms, including suicide ideations and attempts (Taillieu et al., 2022). These phenomena combine, negatively impacting the quality of life in adulthood (Taillieu et al., 2022). Researchers have further posited that there are significant correlations between ACEs and substance misuse, self-harm, and domestic violence (Witt et al., 2021). These ACEs, although experienced in childhood, will manifest in adulthood in some form, from minor to possibly debilitating. Investigation of the contributing factors warrants further consideration (Fisher, 2019; Witt et al., 2021).

Sexual Abuse

Childhood trauma exacerbates mental health function in adult life. One study examined incarcerated women ($n = 212$) who reported having experienced more than one act of physical and sexual abuse (Taillieu et al.,

2022). The results revealed that 61.4% of women experienced physical and sexual abuse (Taillieu et al., 2022). Researchers suggested that the longer a child was exposed to trauma, the more extreme the long-term outcome (Taillieu et al., 2022). Prolonged exposure has demonstrated an increase in the risk of the victim becoming what they have lived, perpetrators of physical violence, necessitating professional trauma-informed interventions to mitigate life-long scarring (Taillieu et al., 2022).

Cyrus et al. (2021) indicated in their study that 28.3% of women reported more than one act of sexual abuse. This experience may lead to PTSD and smoking. Anxiety and other emotional disorders are commonly associated with post-trauma exposure to physical or sexual violence (Fisher, 2019; Sheffler et al., 2022). Mood disorders increase proportionately to the number of ACEs exposure (Fisher, 2019; Sheffler et al., 2022). Additionally, ACEs have been directly correlated to increased depression, suicide attempts, premature hospitalization for mental illness, increased chronic health conditions, and increased risk of homelessness (Sheffler et al., 2022). Fisher (2019) suggested that those affected by the trauma of physical or sexual abuse have experienced difficulties with emotional self-management and develop maladaptive coping such as hypervigilance and anxiety (Sheffler et al., 2022).

Hypervigilance and anxiety are the results of traumatic memory. Fisher posited that the effective management of explicit memories in childhood helps adults form better lifestyles around happy memories (2019). The opposite often occurs as most parents are not equipped to teach children to recognize and capture explicit memories. Therefore, when traumatic events occur in childhood, adults tend to participate in high-risk behavior. Scientists have demonstrated how the amygdala shuts down along with the left frontal cortex, where implicit memories are stored, making people not know when the trauma has ended. This recurring trauma memory traps the affected individual in a repeated state of hypervigilance, and the amygdala responds to stressful stimuli in an unhealthy manner (Fisher, 2019). With this continued dysregulation in mental health function, it is imperative to study the phenomena better to understand the cause-and-effect status of ACEs to outcomes (Fisher, 2019; Taillieu et al., 2022; Witt et al., 2019). What becomes of the child who witnesses physical violence and then becomes the subject of emotional abuse?

Research on ACEs has been consistent in its focus on childhood physical abuse or exposure to the same (Taillieu et al., 2022; Willie et al., 2021). Multiple studies focus on emotional abuse; however, each study investigates emotional abuse and other types of juvenile mistreatments, such as physical, sexual, and emotional mistreatment (Taillieu et al., 2022; Willie et al., 2021). Between 2017 – 2018, researchers in Germany investigated the cumulative outcome effects of childhood maltreatment in adulthood. The participants in the study were at least age 14 ($n = 2531$) and were comprised of 1,401 (55.4%) females and 1,130 (44.6%) males (Witt et al., 2019).

Analysis of odds ratios for combined ACEs showed that the odds risk was comparably lower, as was the number of ACEs (Witt et al., 2019). The preceding year before survey participation, those with no self-reported ACEs indicated lowered odds of developing adult conditions such as depression ($OR = 1.0$), anxiety ($OR = 1.0$), and being physically aggressive ($OR = 1.0$) (Witt et al., 2019). For those with more than four self-reported ACEs, the odds of developing adult conditions such as depression ($OR = 7.79$), anxiety ($OR = 7.09$), and having perpetrated physical violence ($OR = 10.45$) in the past 12 months before the survey were all significant within the 95% confidence interval (Witt et al., 2019). When other ACEs were controlled for, there remained a high cumulative effect in those reporting more than four ACEs compared to those reporting none (Witt et al., 2019).   Witt et al. (2019) explained that psychosocial dysfunction and ACEs negatively impact its victims. When the ACEs were compounded, or more than four were reported, the odds risk increased significantly, strengthening the relationship between the multiple ACEs and the maladaptive behaviors and psychosocial challenges that follow in adulthood (Witt et al., 2019). The literature referenced multiple times the negative outcomes of repeated exposure to not just one but compounded ACEs. The effects of these exposures result in maladaptive behaviors in adulthood, like perpetrated substance use disorder, sexual or physical mistreatment, substance abuse, depression, anxiety, physical aggression, and controlling behaviors (Cyrus et al., 2021; Taillieu et al., 2022; Willie et al., 2021; Witt et al., 2019). As recent as six years ago, researchers suggested that the type of sex crime committed by males has been

associated with higher ACEs scores on the 10-item scale (Taillieu et al.,

2022). As the ACEs score increases, so do the odds of sex crimes becoming

more violent (Taillieu et al., 2022). Some used weapons during the

commission of a crime or injured victims (Taillieu et al., 2022).

Polyvictimization, more than one ACE experienced during childhood, is also

closely associated with increased household dysfunction, including substance

use disorder

(Taillieu et al., 2022).

Household Substance Use

Felitti (2019) described household challenges as parental incarceration,

mental illness among family members, witnessing the mother be physically

or emotionally abused, separation or divorce of the parents, and substance use

disorder. Taillieu et al. (2020) suggested that much research has been

completed on the cumulative and even bivariate effects of ACEs on

household dysfunction. However, there remains a gap in investigating the

effects of individual ACEs types on household dysfunction (Taillieu et al.,

2022). When analyzing the original ACEs study data from Felitti, bivariate

analysis of the variables demonstrated increased victimization related to

substance use disorder (Taillieu et al., 2022). Household substance use

disorder is synonymous with increased socioeconomic challenges and chronic

health difficulties (Westermair et al., 2018). Previous studies have considered individual types of ACEs effects on outcomes in adulthood without accounting for confounding variables (Westermair et al., 2018). In contrast, other studies combined results from multiple questionnaires to receive a quantifiable result for analysis (Westermair et al., 2018).

Research inclusive of Australian women revealed that they had multiple chronic health conditions and high-risk health behaviors that were originally thought attributable to poor health behavior choices such as poor nutrition, smoking, drug use, and lack of activity leading to obesity (Loxton et al., 2021). Upon further analysis, they discovered that those women, despite elevated taxes and punishments regarding the use of illicit drugs, continued to participate in risky behaviors (Loxton et al., 2021). Researchers posited that something more had to influence their decisions to continue their risky behavior choices (Loxton et al., 2021). The more researchers perused the literature, they discovered that household dysfunction related to substance use disorder, mental illness, and incarcerated parents was a growing concern (Loxton et al., 2021). They found that about 46.4% of British citizens in Britain admitted experiencing at least one ACE
(Loxton et al., 2021).

In other countries, they found similar results; 72% from Canada, 82% from Saudi Arabia, and 66% from San Diego in the United States all had participants who admitted experiencing at least one ACE (Loxton et al., 2021). As the researchers continued their investigation, they determined that there were links between the chronic health conditions patients had concerns about and the ACES they were reporting (Loxton et al., 2021). When they looked at the original Felitti study, Loxton et al. (2021) saw the similarities captured in the 1998 data. They investigated the prevalence of physical and emotional disorders previously associated with ACEs (Loxton et al., 2021). Out of the 8607 women who participated in the study, 59% admitted exposure to one ACE, and 26% reported exposure to more than one ACE (Loxton et al., 2021).

The final analysis revealed three main categories of household dysfunction. The most frequently reported ACEs were mental illness (41.4%), second was psychological abuse (24.1%) (Loxton et al., p. 4, 2021), and finally, substance use disorder (24.3%). As the researchers expected, those reporting more than four ACEs had double the number of chronic health and mental health illnesses and reported drug use at more than double the rate of women who reported no ACEs (Loxton et al., 2021). This study lends merit to the suppositions of Taillieu et al. (2022) that more research needs to be conducted on ACEs' influence on substance use disorder as a household dysfunction, both as an individual type and part of multiple ACEs.

Summary and Conclusions

Childhood traumas contribute to mental health disorders and chronic health conditions in adulthood (Taillieu et al., 2022). ACEs have been studied and documented since 1998, demonstrating a dose-response effect from

short-term through long-term exposure to childhood traumas (Felitti, 2019).
The traumas for this study are identified as child sexual mistreatment and
household substance use disorder (Felitti, 2019; Taillieu et al., 2022).
Approximately 36% of women in the United States will be victimized by
sexual violence or other physical trauma (Decker et al., 2019; Jones et al.,
2018). About 21% of women have been documented as victims of sexual
aggression (Decker et al., 2019; Jones et al., 2018). They have displayed
difficulty with academic progression and completion, recidivism, and mental
health issues, which prompts one to wonder if that individual had a history of
domestic violence or other childhood trauma (Nikulina et al., 2021).
Additionally, women whose deaths are attributed to domestic violence rank
43% for women compared to 8% for men. Former significant others are
responsible for half of the homicidal crimes committed against women
(Decker et al., 2019). The more ACEs identified in women, the higher the
odds of those women displaying increased risks of mental health and chronic
health difficulties (Taillieu et al., 2022). For men who commit sex crimes,
this has been corroborated with higher ACEs scores (Taillieu et al., 2022).
The higher the ACEs score, the more violent the sex crimes they commit
become. Polyvictimization is closely linked to increased household
dysfunction and substance use disorder (Taillieu et al., 2022).

The social ecological model is the best framework to theoretically
reconfigure services to match the identified problem. As adolescent females

from these identified homes interact with community agencies such as local departments of social services, schools, and mental health providers, all should be in concert with the employment of the ACEs questionnaire to screen for trauma exposure in the home environment. If positively identified for ACEs and reported mental health concerns, trauma-informed care should be utilized by licensed therapists to engage the family and the child in better managing the resulting behaviors (Fisher, 2019). This is why it is important to accurately consider the research questions and hypotheses utilizing the appropriate analysis methodology.

Chapter 3: Research Method

Introduction

The purpose of this quantitative predictive study was to investigate how the mental health of women with a history of domestic violence is impacted by age, sex, marital status, income, education, employment status, sexual abuse, and substance use disorder. In this chapter, I will review the research design and rationale regarding the identified independent and dependent variables of interest, which will aid in identifying the research design, hypotheses, and questions. There will be a review of why this study design and methodological application will advance public health knowledge of mental health outcomes in women and the complexity of sexual abuse, substance use disorder, and domestic violence. The target population will be clearly defined along with the sampling procedures, reasoning for sample size determination, and alpha levels. The institutional review board (IRB) process will be described in detail, and copies of those permissions are found in Appendix D, Figures 19 and 20.

Research Design and Rationale

For this predictive study design, archival publicly available data were used to compare the individual and combined influences of sexual abuse and substance use disorder on mental health. Multivariate ordinal logistic regression tested for the appropriate correlation of the predictor variables regarding the likelihood of adolescents with individual or combined ACEs developing mental health conditions. Research projects can be structured in many ways. The gold standard is a random controlled trial.
This research requires a lot of time and resources but is anticipated to yield the most beneficial results.

The primary considerations for developing any research project were the variables of interest, how the outcome was to be described, and the project's goal. The variables available for this project were from a secondary data source with one dependent or response variable and multiple independent or predictive categorical variables. As a quantitative study, the most appropriate design is predictive with multivariate ordinal logistic regression to test for association among the variables (Laerd Statistics, n.d.). Others have used similarly structured research designs to investigate associations between variables with statistically significant outcomes.

In this research project, I investigated how sexual abuse and substance use disorder contribute to maladaptive mental health coping of women with a history of domestic violence. It was designed to inform providers of services to children and adolescents about the contributions of ACEs to adulthood concerns of emotional difficulties that may lead to further victimization by domestic violence. The findings are anticipated to add to existing knowledge, enlightening trauma-informed care regarding the challenges facing youth today in hopes that their future adulthood might be positively influenced for better outcomes.

As ACEs are identified, children and adolescents will be provided appropriate trauma-informed care to benefit them as they emerge into adulthood. As adults, they will have developed appropriate coping skills to help them mitigate life circumstances that may lead to continued revictimization. Researchers were interested in investigating how ACEs and mental health difficulties are often reviewed as cumulative ACEs regarding results as adults (Witt et al., 2019). In the study by Witt et al., the outcomes demonstrated that a majority (43.7%) of the respondents indicated one ACE, while fewer than 9% reported more than three (2019). The top identified ACEs included parents' absence from the home (separation, divorce, incarceration), substance use disorder, emotional abuse, and emotional neglect.

Upon investigating these ACEs using a cumulative risk model, the odds ratios indicated that with the cumulation of variables, the chances of negative emotional health functioning were greater (Witt et al., 2019). The unique offering of this research for Germany was that they had inaugural investigations into the frequency of the emotional health disturbances that result from exposure to one or multiple ACEs (Witt et al., 2019). Supporting the core of this research project is the intention of providing a framework for investigating the odds of mental health difficulties that manifest in women, specifically in women with a history of domestic violence after childhood exposure to one or more ACEs.

For this investigative endeavor, the data came from archival data containing the independent, dependent, and covariate variables of interest. The independent variables are age, sex, education level, marital status, income level, employment, sexual abuse, domestic violence in the homes, and substance misuse. The dependent variable from the description of the raw data is mental health. The independent variables of age, sex, education level, marital status, income level, and employment must be considered for analysis (Jones et al., 2018; DeHart, 2007). Previously, researchers have investigated ACEs' influence on mental health using a cumulative risk model. This model has been used to determine the odds of a particular ACE and its association with occurring mental health conditions (Witt et al., 2019). Some posit that the results are more closely aligned with multiple ACEs than individual ACEs (Lian et al., 2022). However, for those investigating ACEs, it is generally done singularly rather than in multiplicity (Lian et al., 2022). The cumulative model assumes accumulation and may not capture individual effects during a specific timeframe (Lian et al., 2022).

Another limitation is the inability to determine the strength of one ACE compared to another (Lian et al., 2022). Using the cumulative risk model does not allow weighting the variables, limiting the ability to say that one variable more than another has a stronger effect on mental health (Lian et al., 2022). Finally, there is no ability to differentiate the resource of one contributing variable over another (Lian et al., 2022).

Because this model is cumulative, all variables are combined for a cumulative outcome (Lian et al., 2022; Tallieu et al., 2022). Despite these limitations, multivariate ordinal logistic regression remains the most widely used statistical test by which to review the influence of the independent (predictor) variables on the dependent (response) variable (Lian et al., 2022; Witt et al., 2019; Tallieu et al., 2022). Each statistical model of analysis has benefits and limitations. It remains the standard measure of the predictive value of ACEs on mental health. The dependent variable in this study is ordinal. The independent variables for this study are categorical. Multivariate ordinal logistic regression will be used to test for the relationships among the variables (Laerd Statistics,

n.d.). This research methodology will provide more detailed information to help with the replication of this investigation by future scholars.

Methodology

Population

The population of interest, women over the age of 18 with and without a history of domestic violence (n = 10,057), is selected from the 2021 BRFSS study conducted in South Carolina 2021 (CDC, 2021). The population selected for the annual survey are participants aged 18 and over who reside in a noninstitutional environment (CDC, 2021). The national study is executed via telephone to gather valuable information on health status, the demographic make-up of the home, the use of health care services, and other community services to meet their health and mental health needs (CDC, 2021). This survey investigates risk behaviors, chronic disease status, and trends in mortality and disability data across the defined geographical areas (CDC, 2021). The BRFSS study investigates residents of all 50 states in the United States, the Washington, DC area, Puerto Rico, Guam, and the US Virgin Islands. (CDC, 2021a). For 2021, Florida was the only exception (CDC, 2021a). Each state has a BRFSS Coordinator who works with the state and community leaders to implement state-specific health initiatives based on the generalized and cumulative survey results (CDC, 2021a).

For the predictive study design, the interest is whether there is an association between variables (Select Statistical Services, 2022). In the case of this research, there is an interest in the predictive value of ACEs and mental health. The outcome data from BRFSS 2021 are reported in weighted percentages. The entire population of female respondents who did or did not identify a history of domestic violence and mental health will be analyzed (n = 10,057). To accurately analyze the effect of the sociodemographic variables on mental health, it was necessary to examine the entire population of women who either did or did not identify any of the ACEs of concern for this research project.

Selecting a smaller sample may have skewed the results (Salkind et al., 2020; Gerstman, 2015). Completing the statistical analysis yielded the odds of the dependent variable presenting with influence from the independent variables (Salkind et al., 2020; Gerstman,

2015). This involved reviewing all independent variables, independently and cumulatively, as they may have affected the variation in the response variable (Gerstman, 2015; Laerd Statistics, n.d.). To determine how the CDC weighted the data, I referenced the appropriate manuals containing this information and have included examples later.

Archival Data Sample Selection Procedures

The BRFSS data were collected in 1984, with only 15 states participating (CDC, 2021). As of 2021, data are collected yearly, focusing on the health and risk behaviors of selected participants from all 50 states (CDC,

2021a). The survey is purposed to gather and analyze data on an aggregated

national level and target related statewide needs (CDC, 2021a). Surveys are

conducted via telephone, both landline and cellular. Participants are randomly

selected and are directed to an adult aged 18 or over in the home (CDC,

2021). Participants must be in a home or college residential setting. The

survey is executed by state health departments via guidance from the CDC as

requested (CDC, 2021). Survey dissemination varies according to each state

and is conducted by health department staff or a third-party company (CDC,

2021).

State health department associates are responsible for storing,

processing, editing, and analyzing the data collected. Each state department

maintains its own database with weighted data and summary statistics

available to the public in various formats (CDC, 2021). In 2021, the

methodology changed from a stratified concept to a ranking, iterative

proportional fitting (CDC, 2021a). This statistical analysis methodology

allows for investigating the demographic information juxtaposed to the

cellular and landline call types (CDC, 2021a). For the purposes of this

research project, this variable is not under review.

> The constitution of the questions utilized in the BRFSS survey is
> comprised of

National Health and Nutrition Examination Survey (NHANES) and the

National Health Interview (NHI) Survey (CDC, 2021a). South Carolina and

other states selected the inclusion of the ACEs Questionnaire (CDC, 2021a).

Each state utilizes the core component questions that investigate health conditions, caregiving, risk behavior status, mental health status, basic demographic information, and nutritional information (CDC, 2021). Then, each state has the option to select additional modules that investigate such health concerns as sun exposure, diabetes or prediabetic dietary behaviors, cancer diagnoses in families, and other nervous system illnesses such as shingles (CDC, 2021). Once the state has reviewed, revised, and edited its questionnaire, it is forwarded to the CDC for review and approval before the survey is completed (CDC, 2021a). Using landlines and cellular phone lines allows for greater inclusion of participants (CDC, 2021a).

The population for participation in the survey is selected via a probability sample of eligible households using telephones in South Carolina (CDC, 2021a). The Department of Social Services (DSS) employs a stratification system that groups phone numbers into two groups or strata (CDC, 2021a). Using a probability-based algorithm, the data selection for cellular phone numbers is based on a combination derived from the prefix and the first two numbers of the phone number until the first block of 100 numbers is confirmed for contact (CDC, 2021a). Landline phone numbers for contact are based on a similar probability sample technique where the numbers are divided into blocks of 1,000 (CDC, 2021a). From that block of 1,000, a phone number is randomly selected for contact (CDC, 2021a). To maintain confidentiality, any identifying information, such as specific information on race, ethnicity, and those over the age of 80, was removed for the year of the survey (CDC, 2021a).

Interview Selection Process

In 2021, 50 states participated in the BRFSS project (CDC, 2021a). The data collection method was a computer-assisted phone interview system (WinCATI software) that allowed for ease of data collection (CDC, 2021a). The average interview time was 17 minutes, with an additional 5–10 minutes for additional modules selected by states (CDC, 2021a). Oversight of call quality was monitored according to BRFSS standards. Each state has a BRFSS Coordinator to oversee the hiring, training, retention, quality improvement, and execution of the survey (CDC, 2021a). Because the CDC has a call quality requirement installed with the employment of BRFSS, all interviewers' calls are closely monitored either on-site or from a remote location (CDC, 2021a). Calls monitored are determined by the amount of call time of each interviewer; in some cases, calls are made to the interviewee to review the accuracy of the interviewer (CDC, 2021a). Call frequency was 7 days a week: morning, afternoon, and evening (CDC, 2021a). For more details on the response rates from 2021, the Summary Data Quality Report is available by request (CDC, 2021a).

Data Request Process

South Carolina began collecting BRFSS ACE data in 2014 (CDC, 2021a). To access the data, the state BRFSS Coordinator must be contacted

(CDC, 2021). The SC BRFSS Coordinator who is an employee of the SC

Department of Health and

Environmental Control (SC DHEC) in the Division of Surveillance at the

Bureau of Health Improvement and Equity (CDC, 2021) was emailed

regarding the specific steps to be completed regarding access to the data for

South Carolina for only the questions of interest to answer the research

questions and hypotheses (CDC, 2021). Expedited approval accompanied the

proposal idea, research questions, hypotheses, and IRB approval.

Operationalization of the Variables

Felitti originally proposed 10 ACEs in the 1998 study. Child abuse was

defined as emotional, physical, and sexual mistreatment (Afifi, 2022). There

were five types of household dysfunction: household substance use disorder,

incarceration, emotional difficulties, separation of a parent through divorce or

separation, and violence against the mother (Afifi, 2022). This study has nine

independent (predictor) variables: age, sex, income level, education,

employment, marital status, sexual abuse, domestic violence, and substance

use disorder. The dependent (response) variable is mental illness.

The data were organized for female responses via landline (LANDSEX

= 2) AND cell phone (CELLSEX = 2) (CDC et al., 2021). Because question

number three in core section number two combines the respondent's

perception of their physical or emotional health over the past month, it may

be considered a confounding variable, which will be accounted for before data analysis later in this section (CDC et al., 2021). The following tables

provide the module questions and details, helping identify how the CDC

operationalized the variables. The BRFSS questionnaire has three ACE

questions to identify this variable. *Note.* Figure 2 demonstrates how sexual

abuse was ascertained.

Figure 2

Sexual Abuse Operationalized

Module Questions	Module Details
1. **How often did anyone at least five years older than you or an adult ever touch you sexually?**	a. Module number 20, question 9 – How often did anyone ever touch you sexually (CDC et al., pp. 111 – 112, 2021)?
2. **How often did anyone at least five** – **years older than you or an adult try to** make you touch **make you touch them sexually?**	a. Module number 20, question 10 How often did anyone them sexually (CDC et al., pp. 111 – 112, 2021)?
3. **How often did anyone at least five years older than you or an adult force you to have sex?**	a. Module number 20, question 11 – How often did anyone ever force you to have sex (CDC et al., pp. 111 – 112, 2021)? b. Responses options: 1 = Never, 2 = Once, 3 = More than once, 7 = Don't know/ not sure, 9 = Refused, Blank = Not asked or missing (CDC et al., pp. 111 – 112, 2021).

Note. To investigate substance use disorder, the survey utilized two ACE

questions as found in Figure 3.

Figure 3

Substance Use Disorder Operationalized

Module Questions	Module Details
1. **Did you live with anyone who was a problem drinker or alcoholic?**	a. Module number 20, question 2 – Live with a problem drinker/alcoholic (CDC et al., pp. 107 – 106, 2021)?
2. **Did you live with anyone who** question 3 **used illegal street drugs or** who used **who abused prescription medications?**	a. Module number 20, – Live with anyone illegal drugs or abused prescriptions (CDC et al., pp. 107 – 106, 2021)? b. Responses options: 1 = Yes, 2 = No, 7 = Don't know/ not sure, 9 = Refused, Blank = Not asked or missing (CDC et al., pp. 107 – 106, 2021).

Note. To investigate mental health involvement, the BRFSS survey tool investigated mental health outside of the ACE factors questionnaire. The following questions in

Figure 4 were posed using a Likert scale.

Figure 4

Mental Health Operationalized

Module Questions	Module Details

Module Questions	Module Details
1. **Now thinking about your mental health, which includes stress, depression, and problems with emotions, for how many days during the past 30 days was your mental health not good?**	a. Section name: Healthy Days, question number 2 - Number of days mental health not good (CDC et al., pp. 20 – 21, 2021).
2. **During the past 30 days, for** Days, **about how many days did** Healthy **poor physical or mental health keep you from doing** the **your usual activities, such as** None, 77 **self-care, work, or recreation?**	a. Section name: Healthy question number 3 – days b. Response options: 1-30 = number of days, 88 = = Don't know/ not sure, 99 = Refused, Blank = Not asked or missing (CDC et al., pp. 20 – 21, 2022). c. To distinguish between physical and mental health in question 2, a note is added: for "section 02.01, PHYSHLTH is 88 and section 2.02, MENTHLTH is 88 (CDC et al., pp. 20 – 21, 2021).

Confounding Variables Operationalized

To address potential confounding variables, the following variables were considered for analysis. Using a Likert scale, the following questions captured the responses. *Note.* Questions about age were collected according to landline or cell phone use and are provided below for review in Figure 5.

Figure 5

Age Operationalized

Module Questions	**Module Details**

Module Questions	Module Details
1. Are you 18 years of age or older?	a. Section name: Landline introduction
	b. Response options: Yes = 1 c. No = 2, terminate phone call d. Blank = Not asked or missing (CDC et al., p. 11, 2021).
2. Are you 18 years of ag or older? introduction	a. Section name: Cell phone introduction b. Response options: Yes = 1 c. Blank = Not asked or missing (CDC et al., p. 15, 2021).

Note. Sex was queried according to the type of phone used during the call.

The module questions and details are found in Figure 6 below.

Figure 6

Sex Operationalized by Gender

Module Questions	Module Details
1. Are you male or female?	a. Section name: Landline Introduction b. Response Options: Male = 1 c. Female = 2 d. Blank = Not asked or missing (CDC et al., p. 16, 2021).
2. Are you male or introduction	a. Section name: Landline **female?** b. Response options: Male = 1 c. Female = 2 d. Don't know/Not sure = 7 (terminate phone call) e. Refused = 9 (terminate phone call) f. Blank = Not asked or missing (CDC et al., p. 12, 2021).

 To determine the sex of the respondent completing the survey, the following question in Figure 7 was asked.

Figure 7

Sex Operationalized by Phone Type

Module Question	Module Details
1. **Sex of respondent**	a. Section Name: Respondent Sex b. Response options: Male = 1 if LANDSEX = 1 or CELLSEX = 1 or COLGSEX = 1 c. Female = 2 if LANDSEX = 2 or CELLSEX = 2 or COLGSEX = 2 (CDC et al., p. 19, 2021).

Note. To investigate the level of education attained by the respondent, the following question in Figure 8 was provided.

Figure 8

Education Level Operationalized

Module Question	Module Details
1. What is the highest grade or year of school you completed?	a. Section name: Demographics b. Response Options: Never attended school or only kindergarten = 1 c. Grades 1 through 8 (Elementary) = 2 d. Grades 9 through 11 (Some high school) = 3 e. Grade 12 or GED (High school graduate) = 4 f. College 1 year to 3 years (Some college or technical school = 5 g. College 4 years or more (College graduate) = 6 h. Refused = 9 i. Blank = Not asked or missing (CDC et al., p. 37, 2021).

Note. To investigate employment status, the following question in Figure 9 was provided.

Figure 9

Employment Operationalized by Status

Module Question	Module Details
1. Are you currently employed?	a. Section Name: Demographics b. Response options: Employed for wages = 1 c. Self-employed = 2 d. Out of work for 1 year or more = 3 e. Out of work for < 1 year = 4 f. A homemaker = 5 g. A student = 6 h. Retired = 7 i. Unable to work = 8 j. Refused = 9 k. Blank = Not asked or missing (CDC et al., p. 41, 2021).

Note. To investigate income, the following question in Figure 10 was provided.

Figure 10

Income Operationalized

Module Question	Module Details
1. Is your annual household income from all sources: (If respondent refuses at any income level, code 'Refused.')	a. Section name: Demographics b. Response Options: Less than $10,000 = 1 c. Less than $15,000 ($10,000 to < $15,000) = 2 d. Less than $20,000 ($15,000 to <$20,000) = 3 e. Less than $25,000 ($20,000 to < $25,000 = 4

f. Less than $35,000
($25,000 to < $35000) =
5
g. Less than $50,000
($35,000 to < $50,000) =
6
h. Less than $75,000
($50,000 to < $75,000) =
7

i. Less than $100,000 ($75,000 to < $100,000) = 8
j. Less than $150,000

($100,000 to < $150,000) = 9

k. Less than $200,000

($150,000 to < $200,000) =

10
l. $200,000 or more = 11
m. Don't know/not sure = 77
n. Refused = 99 (CDC et al., p.
41, 2021).

Note. A review of the participant's marital status was captured using the following questions in Figure 11.

Figure 11

Marital Status

Module Question	**Module Details**
1. **Are you: (marital status)**	a. Section name: demographics b. Response options: Married = 1 c. Divorced = 2 d. Widowed = 3 e. Separated = 4 f. Never married = 5 g. A member of an unmarried couple = 6 h. Refused = 9 i. Blank = Not asked or missing (CDC et al. p. 36, 2021).

Note. An example of the overall analysis from the codebook, as indicated by CDC et al.

(2021) for Question Number 2, is included in Figure 12 below.

Figure 12

Sample Analysis of BRFSS Question 2.0

Question Number: 2
Column: 104-105
Type of Variable: Num
SAS Variable Name: MENTHLTH
Question Prologue:
Question: Now thinking about your mental health, which includes stress, depression, and problems with emotions, for how many days during the past 30 days was your mental health not good?

Value	Value Label	Frequency	Percentage	Weighted Percentage
1 - 30	Number of days Notes: _ _ Number of days	159,615	36.38	39.85
88	None	271,161	61.81	58.38
77	Don't know/Not sure	5,723	1.30	1.27
99	Refused	2,192	0.50	0.49
BLANK	Not asked or Missing	2	.	.

Data Analysis Plan

IBM SPSS Statistics Version 28 was used for data analysis. Once access to the data was provided, the data was transferred to an Excel spreadsheet for scrubbing. Once the data was scrubbed to ensure its appropriateness to answer the research questions and that blank or no responses have been accounted for, the data was ready for input to SPSS for analysis (Salkind et al., 2020). From the variable view in SPSS, the variables were labeled and set up according to their type (Salkind et al., 2020). The dependent variable, mental health, was set up as ordinal. The independent variables of age, sex, education level, marital status, income level, employment, sexual abuse, domestic violence in the homes, and substance misuse were identified as categorical. Mental health was used as the ordinal dependent variable.

Once obtained, the data were scrubbed for all female respondents who responded to the following: age, sex, education level, marital status, income level, employment, sexual abuse, substance use, mental health, and domestic violence in the home, as those respondents, were the target population for the study ($n = 10,057$) (CDC et al., 2021). It was imperative to have a comparison group for the purposes of odds ratio calculations. Therefore, the analysis included those who acknowledged mental health issues and a history of domestic violence among those who did not (Gerstman, 2015).

The CDC reported the outcomes from the questionnaire in weighted percentages (CDC, 2022a). This was taken into consideration when performing the analysis to avoid skewed results (CDC, 2022a). Prior to completing any analysis, all manuals providing information on the weighting of the main and optional modules utilized were downloaded (CDC, 2022a). Making sure to avoid duplication, the data was available to be downloaded from a central repository (2022a). Information from the main modules containing demographic information was weighted, and the code _LLCPWT was utilized to designate those variables (CDC, 2022a; CDC, 2022b). *Note.* Figure 13 below provides more information on the module weighting by land line and cell phone for the state of South Carolina.

Figure 13

Weighted Modules by State

Modules by State				
State	Description	Data Set	Data Weight	Module(s)
South Carolina	Combined Land Line and Cell Phone data	LLCP2021	_LLCPWT	Adverse Childhood Experiences, Caregiver, Pre-Diabetes

Based on Figure 13, coding was entered in SPSS to note the variance with the main variables and the ACEs variables (CDC, 2022b). After the variables were appropriately designated, multivariate ordinal logistic regression analysis was run in SPSS (Laerd Statistics, n.d.) to address the research questions and related hypotheses. The research questions follow.

RQ1: What is the relationship between mental health and age, sex, and education of women with or without a history of domestic violence?

H_{10}: There will be no relationship between mental health and age, sex, and education of women with a history of domestic violence.

H_{1a}: There will be a relationship between mental health and age, sex, and education of women with a history of domestic violence.

RQ2: What is the relationship between mental health and marital status, income level, and employment in women with or without a history of domestic violence?

H_{20}: There will be no relationship between mental health and marital status, income level, and employment in women with a history of domestic violence.

H_{2a}: There will be a relationship between mental health and marital status, income level, and employment in women with a history of domestic violence.

RQ3: What is the relationship between mental health and sexual abuse, and substance use disorder in women with and without a history of domestic violence?

H_{30}: There will be no relationship between mental health and sexual

abuse and substance use disorder in women with a history of domestic

violence.

H_{3a}: There will be a relationship between mental health and sexual

abuse and substance use disorder in women with a history of domestic

violence. *Note.* Figure 14 depicts the effects of the nine independent

categorical variables on the ordinal dependent variable mental health.

Figure 14

Diagram of Variable Effects

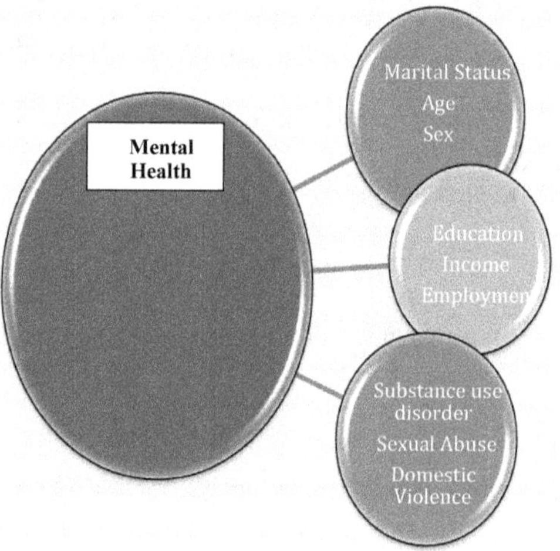

Multivariate ordinal logistic regression was the most appropriate

statistical test for the hypotheses (Laerd Statistics, n.d.). This was most

appropriate as the desire was to predict a relationship among the identified

independent variables and the ordinal dependent variable (Laerd Statistics,

n.d.). Using multivariate ordinal logistic regression allowed for the investigation of relationships between each independent variable and the cumulation of those variables and their effect, if any, on the dependent variable (Laerd Statistics, n.d.). It allowed for investigating the predictive power of multivariate ordinal logistic regression on the dependent variable (Laerd Statistics, n.d.). Another benefit to using multivariate ordinal logistic regression was the ability to investigate further how the predictor and response variables were complementary (Laerd Statistics, n.d.). The response variable was reported as a cumulative odds ratio, as the interest was in the predictive value of the independent variables to the response variable (Laerd Statistics, n.d.).

Assumptions and Confounding Variables

According to Laerd Statistics (n.d.), four assumptions must be met for variables to qualify for ordinal logistic regression statistical analysis. The first assumption is that there is one ordinal dependent variable (Laerd Statistics, n.d.; Salkind & Frey, 2021). Although the independent variables in the study are represented on a Likert scale, they were treated as categorical data (Laerd Statistics, n.d.; Gerstman, 2015). The third assumption is the avoidance of multicollinearities. This assumes the categorical predictive variables are too closely related to determining which is a stronger predictor variable. Laerd Statistics (n.d.) suggests running a test in SPSS using dummy variables to rule this out. Procedural guidance is provided by Laerd Statistics (n.d.) on how to complete this computation in SPSS and interpret the results. One potential confounding independent variable for the outcomes was mental health combined with physical health in one question. Because there was no way to tease out the physical health component of this question, it was not selected for analysis. Other independent variables considered were age, sex, income level, education, marital status, and employment. These indicate that each variable has proportional odds of cumulatively affecting the dependent variable.

It is suggested to separate binomial logistic regressions on cumulative dichotomous dependent variables (Laerd Statistics, p.8, n.d.) to determine further compliance with this assumption. The test for multicollinearity was completed and shared in the following chapter.

Threats to Validity

Beginning with 15 states in 1984, the BRFSS Questionnaire is now annually employed in 51 states (CDC et al., 2021). The BRFSS Questionnaire has three main sections: a main module, selected options, and state-preferred questions (CDC et al., 2021). The main modules are questions related to health-related conditions, perceived health care provided, risk behavior participation such as smoking, tobacco use, and HIV/AIDS risk status (CDC et al., 2021). This core section comprises questions queried annually and other questions that rotate on odd and even years (CDC et al., 2021). The questionnaire comprises questions extracted from national surveys (CDC et al., 2021). The national surveys have been tested for validity and reliability (CDC et al., 2021). The state-based results utilizing these questions in the core and optional modules can be compared to the national responses (CDC et al., 2021).

Secondary data, such as the BRFSS, is convenient for a graduate student to use as it can come in the form of big data collected by larger national organizations, such as the case here. Due to numerous variables often contained in secondary data, there are extensive possibilities to collect information for various methods of inquiry, hypothesizing, and formulating research questions (Weston et al., 2019). Because this data has been collected using validated and reliable instruments on a large enough scale, upon reproduction, the methodology will be generalizable to the larger population (Weston et al., 2019). States devising independent questions must be tested for validity and reliability and are subsequently tested among a select population (CDC et al., 2021).

Those questions are only permitted for use after approval by a majority vote among the

State BRFSS Coordinators. (CDC et al., 2021)

The optional modules cover topics such as diabetes, nutritional intake of excess sugar, environmental exposures, autoimmune disorders, and cancer diagnoses of family members. The BRFSS Coordinators work closely together to determine which optional questions will be included in the optional module (CDC et al., 2021). Finally, the CDC does not review, track, or report on state-based questions (CDC et al., 2021).

To address external validity, the BRFSS Coordinators hire and train all interviewers (CDC et al., 2021). The interviewers are to read all questions from a script verbatim and must refrain from elaborating on any questions to assist an interviewee in answering the question (CDC et al., 2021). For the survey year 2021, the CDC et al (2021) approved 28 modules. However, to better manage the survey length and time for responses, each state chose the state-related questions carefully (CDC et al., 2021).

For the states that add their state-specific questions, after approval, those questions are combined with the core and optional modules and forwarded to the CDC, which then stores a copy in an archived file on their website for one calendar year (CDC et al., 2021). The CDC provides translation of the core and optional modules, with each state bearing responsibility for translating state-specific questions (CDC et al., 2021). It should be noted that translation may be adapted for the majority Latino population in that state (CDC et al., 2021).

Ethical Considerations

Participants must be selected for participation in a systematic manner. The hypotheses are used to test statistical significance stemming from the research question. The population must be sampled such that some inference may be drawn from the population for statistical analysis (Gerstman, 2015). The CDC, since 2011, has conducted telephone surveys from respondents who are given information about the purpose of the survey, who is conducting the survey, and for what purpose (CDC et al., 2021). Each interviewer also allows the participant to discontinue participation to any question or at any time during the survey administration (CDC et al., 2021). Survey information is captured and entered absent of identifying demographic information (CDC et al., 2021). All forms used to collect data are approved by the OMB and have an approval number readily available to the respondent (CDC et al., 2021). Should a respondent have questions that the interviewer needs clarification on, there is a CDC staff person available for consultation (CDC et al., 2021). The interviewer verifies the phone number and whether it is a landline or a cell phone number (CDC et al., 2021). The age, sex, and verification of the person answering the call as an adult residing in the household are also confirmed (CDC et al., 2021). At no time are any identifying pieces of information requested or gathered (CDC et al., 2021).

The CDC and BRFSS have devised a Research Request Application for South

Carolina to be completed and then forwarded along with the completed and approved IRB from Walden University. Upon an average six-week review and approval period, permission to access the data electronically is granted. The data is available for a specified amount of time. Once that granted period has closed, access to the data is once again restricted. Only the specific data needed for completing the analysis will be available. Once the researcher has completed the use of the data, it must then be confidentially disposed of according to CDC protocol which will be shared when the data is made available (CDC et al., 2021). The researcher has no known personal conflicts or interests that would bias the project. Walden University has provided Institutional Review Board (IRB) approval along with the SCDHEC for conducting the research project (Appendix D, Figure 19; Appendix D, Figure 20).

Summary

It is the hope of this research to investigate how sexual abuse and substance use disorder predict the mental health functioning of women with a history of domestic violence. By investigating the relationships between sexual abuse and substance use disorder on the mental health of women while accounting for potential confounding variables, the desire is to provide improved assessments of children to look more universally for ACEs and improve the delivery of services to begin to make a difference for them as emerging adults. It is also hoped that the outcomes will provide a basis for public health policy development or revision for services currently geared to children and women with children who have similarly identified attributes to this project.

Using multivariate ordinal logistic regression will allow one to determine the odds of the independent variables' effect on the dependent variable Laerd Statistics, n.d.; Salkind et al., 2020). Thus, providing the odds of developing a mental health condition as an adult after ACEs exposure during childhood (Laerd Statistics, n.d.). Because the BRFSS data is presented in weighted percentages, it is necessary to use the complete sample size of females who responded with or without a history of domestic violence in the home for the purpose of comparison. Accessing valid, consistent, and reliable data collected by the CDC and the State of South Carolina is time and cost-effective (CDC et al., 2021). The stringent management and execution of the BRFSS questionnaire allow data analysis to be completed using valuable data relevant to the ACEs of concern for this project. The final multivariate ordinal logistic regression analysis will allow inference from the population to assist in knowledgeable public health policy development.

Chapter 4: Results

Introduction

I investigated how the mental health of women with a history of domestic violence is impacted by age, sex, marital status, income, education, employment status, sexual abuse, and substance use disorder. The premise proposed is to provide women with the tools and services necessary to help them mitigate the effects of childhood trauma that can manifest in adulthood.

Abstract of Chapter 4

To determine if any independent variables of interest affect the outcome or dependent variable, the plan was to investigate these relationships using multivariate ordinal regression. Upon receipt of the dataset, age, sex, education, and income were identified as scale. The variables of marital status, employment, sexual abuse, domestic violence in the homes, and substance misuse were identified as nominal. By investigating the variable impacts on the dependent variable, I propose that there are variables from those identified that would determine, to a reasonable degree, how a woman's mental health status (depression, stress, and emotional problems) is impacted from those experiences in childhood.

Deviation From the Planned Analysis

The dataset came from the CDC BRFSS. Because the data are weighted, research from the South Carolina 2021 Codebook Report (CDC,

2021) Weighting Description 2021 (CDC, 2021) and the Complex Sampling Weights and Preparing 2021 BRFSS

Module Data for Analysis (CDC, 2022). Upon investigating these manuals and meeting with methodology and statistician advising, it was discovered that a slightly different analysis would need to be computed to account for the specific stratified and population sampling with phone weights. The method of completing the analysis was modified from multivariate ordinal logistic regression to ordinal logistic regression using complex samples.

Data Collection

South Carolina began collecting BRFSS ACE data in 2014 (CDC, 2021). To access the data, the state BRFSS Coordinator, Avalos, was contacted via email regarding the specific steps to be completed regarding access to the data for South Carolina for only the questions of interest to answer the research questions and hypotheses (CDC, 2021). Avalos is the SC BRFSS Coordinator and is an employee of the SC Department of Health and Environmental Control (SC DHEC) in the Division of Surveillance at the Bureau of Health Improvement and Equity (CDC, 2021). The data request application was completed and forwarded to Carlos for review and approval; then, the approved response was received and forwarded to Walden University IRB for recording. A subsequent amendment to the proposed analysis was submitted for one missing variable and was approved.

The requested dataset ($n = 10{,}057$) was transmitted via a secured file in SAS7bdat format through a secured server. That format was transformed into CSV, uploaded into an Excel spreadsheet, and exported to SPSS for analysis.

Data Cleaning

Once obtained, the data were reviewed for completeness. The values for each variable were designated, including blank or refusal responses. The ordinal variable for the number of days mental health was not good (MENTHLTH) was transformed into the same variable from calendar days to categorical data. Low incorporated days one to nine. Medium incorporated days 10 to 19. High incorporated days 20 to 30. The ratio-level independent variables of income, education, and age were not transformed to maintain their strength for regression analysis. Their measurements were set at scale for SPSS data analysis (Laerd Statistics, n.d.).

Sex was coded male and female, then filtered for females as a nominal measurement. The ACEs variables were recoded into the same variable as nominal measurements. Marital status was recoded into the same variable and set as a nominal measurement. The weighted measurements were not transformed, and the measurements remained scale. Because the original data set received ($n = 10{,}057$) was scrubbed for all female respondents who responded to the following: age, sex, education level, marital status, income level, employment, sexual abuse, substance use, mental health, and domestic violence in the home, the population for the study ($n = 4{,}490$) remained a large enough representative sample of the general population ($N = 1,295,788$)

to draw inference (CDC et al., 2021).

Population

The population of interest, women with and without a history of

domestic violence ($n = 10,057$), was selected from the 2021 BRFSS study

conducted in South Carolina 2021 (CDC, 2021a). The population selected for

the annual survey were participants aged 18 and over who reside in a non-

institutional environment (CDC,

2021a).

Descriptive Statistics of the Data Set

For the predictive study design, the interest was an association between

variables (Select Statistical Services, 2022). In the case of this research, there

was an interest in the predictive value of ACEs and mental health. The

outcome data from BRFSS 2021 was reported in weighted percentages. The

entire population of female respondents who did or did not identify a history

of domestic violence and mental health was analyzed ($n = 10,057$). The

respondents ranged in age from 18 to 99, with the age group 65 – 99

possessing the greatest frequency ($n = 1,919$), followed by the age group 55 –

64 ($n = 820$), 45 – 54 ($n = 695$), 35 – 44 ($n = 513$), 25 – 34 ($n = 347$), and 18

– 24 ($n = 196$). A pie graph depicting how the age groups were comprised

and the count for each age group completing the questionnaire is in Appendix

A, Figure 17.

To accurately analyze the effect of the sociodemographic variables on mental health, it was necessary to examine the entire population of women who did or did not identify any of the ACEs of concern for this research project. Selecting a smaller sample may have skewed the results (Gerstman, 2015; Salkind et al., 2020). Completing the statistical analysis yielded the odds of the dependent variable presenting with influence from the independent variables (Gerstman, 2015; Salkind et al., 2020). This involved reviewing all independent variables, independently and cumulatively, as they could have affected the variation in the response variable (Gerstman, 2015; Laerd Statistics, n.d.).

The CDC (2022a) reported the outcomes from the questionnaire in weighted percentages. This was considered when analyzing to avoid skewed results (CDC, 2022a). Before completing the analysis, all manuals providing information on the weighting of the main and optional modules utilized were downloaded (CDC, 2022a). The data was downloaded from a central repository and forwarded via a secure server to avoid duplication. Information from the main modules containing demographic information was weighted. To account for the weighting of the variables, the _LLCPWT weight was utilized with the landline and cellular phone types. To allow for inference from the general population, _@PSU (population strata unit) was incorporated during the analysis. Finally, _@STSR (sample design stratification sample) was used to ensure even sampling from the general population (CDC, 2022a; CDC, 2022b). The survey was conducted statewide for South Carolina, with 358,899 participants completing the survey. Partial responses were 79,794. The population of interest includes all women from the ACEs module participating in the survey who did or did not identify a history of domestic violence. Therefore, $n = 10,057$.

Because the archival data set was derived from a national database, it was best practice to consider all the weighting variables associated with the data set (Banerjee, 2022). Therefore, a complex sample plan was developed in SPSS to accurately complete the ordinal logistic regression (Banerjee, 2022b). Using the correctly weighted variables allowed for the appropriate statistical analysis of the general population (Banerjee, 2022b). Complex samples also compensated for over or under-sampling the selected population (Banerjee, 2022a).

In this chapter, statistical assumptions of the tests of appropriateness for ordinal logistic regression are discussed along with the demographic characteristics of the population of interest, a justification of the independent variables included in the model, complete descriptive statistics, and statistical analysis. The analyses were completed for each research question with a description of the statistical tests of the hypotheses and appropriate illustrations to support the study outcomes.

Data Analysis

Assumption 1

Ordinal regression requires four assumptions to be met. The first requires at least one dependent variable (Laerd Statistics, n.d.). The dependent variable of mental health (number of days that mental health is not good) was transformed into ordinal from days of the month starting with one and ending with thirty. The categories were low (Days 1 to 9), medium (Days 10 to 19), and high (Days 20 to 30).

Assumption 2

The second assumption to be met was having one or more independent variables (Laerd Statistics, n.d.). This study has eight independent variables: age, sex, education, marital status, employment, education level, substance use disorder, and sex abuse.

Assumption 3

Ordinal regression requires a third assumption to be met. Determining the relationships among the variables was important, as multicollinearity had to be ruled out (Laerd Statistics, n.d.). Because three independent variables are scale (continuous), the test for multicollinearity was completed. With Tolerance values greater than 0.1 (the lowest is .339), this indicated a VIF value lower than 10 (the highest is 2.95); therefore, no multicollinearity was detected among the data set (Laerd Statistics, n.d.).

Assumption 4

The final assumption assessed the overall model fit and the ability of the model to predict similar outcomes for individuals from the population who would meet similar characteristics as defined by the independent variables (Laerd Statistics, n.d.). The proportional odds to test for model fit was also an option (Laerd Statistics, n.d.). To assess model fit, the aggregate function was used in SPSS to investigate the cell frequency based on the dependent variable of three levels (Laerd Statistics, n.d.). The recommended cell frequency should be above five. Based on the aggregate review, only one cell (532) had a frequency of less than five ($n = 3.47$). All others were well above that, indicating that the model was a good fit. The one cell with a frequency of $n = 3.47$ served as a reminder to review outcomes related to widowed females with no days that mental health was not good and no positive responses to any independent variables, which had to be interpreted cautiously (Laerd Statistics, n.d.). There were 712 different combinations among the independent variables.

Using complex sample ordinal logistic regression, the dependent variable was dummy coded for ordinal processing in the order of low ($1 - 9$ days), medium ($10 - 19$ days), and high ($20 - 30$ days). Income, education level, and age group were continuous (scale) independent variables. The remaining independent variables were categorical (nominal). After the variables were appropriately prepared for analysis, complex samples ordinal regression analysis was run in SPSS (Laerd Statistics, n.d.) to address the research questions and related hypotheses. The research questions follow.

Research Question 1

What is the relationship between mental health and age, sex, and education of women with or without a history of domestic violence?

H_{10}: There will be no relationship between mental health and age, sex, and education of women with a history of domestic violence.

H_{1a}: There will be a relationship between mental health and age, sex, and education of women with a history of domestic violence.

Data Analysis Plan for Research Question 1

The analysis plan for the first question was to investigate whether age, sex, or education impacted women's mental health with or without a history of domestic violence. In keeping with the standards of best practice documented in the literature review, this question was investigated regarding the contributions of the predictor variables' cumulative and individual impact.

Assumptions for Data Analysis Plan for Research Question 1

I hypothesized that a woman's mental health would be adversely affected after childhood exposure to trauma. Relative to this question, the assumption was that there would be a relationship between age, education, and gender that should impact mental health as defined by the CDC; depression, stress, or emotional problems (CDC, 2021).

Descriptive Statistics for Research Question 1

The sample size for this analysis ($n = 4,490$) represented about 1.3 million respondents ($N = 1,295,788$). As education increased by one level, the dependent variable days of mental health not good decreased. The p-value for this variable was statistically significant ($<.001$). As a result, there were lower odds of education impacting days of mental health not good in women with a history of domestic violence ($OR = .70$, 95% CI - .600 to .817).

The increase in age was associated with a decrease in the dependent variable days of mental health not good ($OR = .823$, 95% CI - .755 to .897). The p-value was statistically significant ($<.001$). Therefore, there were lower odds of age influencing the days that mental health is not good.

As domestic violence experienced in the home during childhood increased, mental health days not good decreased ($OR = .423$, 95% CI - .297 to .603). Therefore, those with no childhood exposure to domestic violence in the home had a lower chance of experiencing days of mental health not good compared to those with greater exposure to domestic violence in the home ($OR = .945$, 95% CI - .557 to 1.60). Based on the Nagelkerke pseudo R^2 value (.083), 8.3% of the variance in the response was attributed to the predictors in the model compared to the null model. Thus, the null hypothesis was rejected

(Salkind et al., 2020). *Note:* Table 1 provides information on the parameter estimates from the ordinal regression analysis.

Table 1

Parameter Estimates for Mental Health, Domestic Violence, Age, and Education

Parameter	B	t	p	Exp(B)	95% CI	95% CI		
							(Lower)	(Upper)
Days mental health not good (1-9)	-.637	2.048	.041	.529			.287	.973
Days mental health not good (10-19)	.020	.065	.948	1.02	.560	1.86		
Domestic violence never	-.860	-.506	<.001	.423	.297	.603		
Domestic violence once Domestic	-.056 .000	-.209	.834	.945 1.00	.557	1.60		
violence more than						.897		
once Age	-.195	-4.44	<.001	.823	.755	.817		
Education	-.357	-4.52	<.001	.700	.600			

According to the overall model effect, a relationship existed between mental health, age, sex, and education of women with or without a history of domestic violence (Appendix A, Table 3). Reviewing the associations of the independent and outcome variables, parameter estimates allowed an inference that variation among the variables was not due to chance but represented an interaction among the variables (Salkind et al., 2020). *Note.* In Figure 15 below, the predictors demonstrated that as the education level of a female with a history of domestic violence increased, the number of days her mental health was not good decreased.

Figure 15

Education and Domestic Violence Predictions on Mental Health

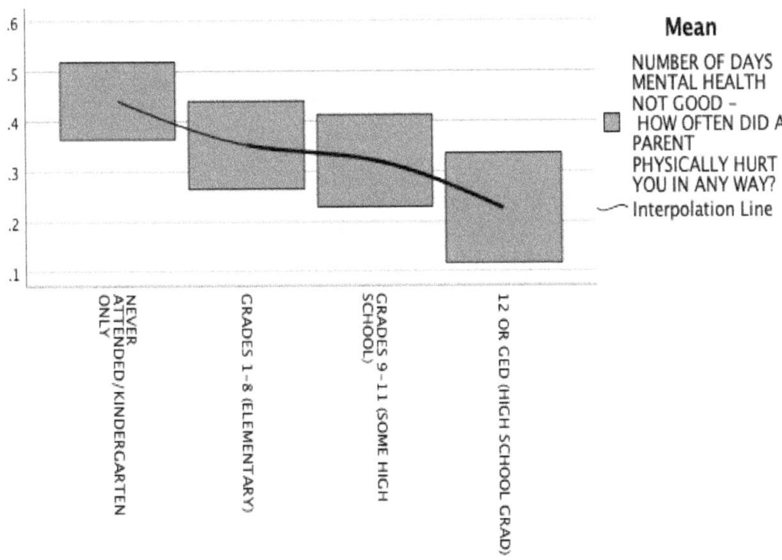

Research Question 2

What is the relationship between mental health and marital status,
income level, and employment in women with or without a history of
domestic violence?

H_{20}: There will be no relationship between mental health and marital
status, income level, and employment in women with a history of domestic
violence.

H_{2a}: There will be a relationship between mental health and marital
status, income level, and employment in women with a history of domestic
violence.

Data Analysis Plan for Research Question 2

The analysis plan for the second question was to investigate whether
marital status, income, or employment impacted women's mental health with

or without a history of domestic violence. This question was investigated regarding the contributions of the predictor variables' cumulative and individual impacts.

Assumptions for Data Analysis Plan for Research Question 2

I hypothesized that a woman's mental health would be adversely affected after childhood exposure to trauma. Relative to this question, the assumption was that a relationship between marital status, employment, and income would impact mental health as defined by the CDC (2021): depression, stress, or emotional problems (Appendix B, Table 4).

Descriptive Statistics for Research Question 2

This analysis's sample size ($n = 4{,}490$) represented about 1 million respondents ($N = 1{,}040{,}654.291$). Based on the pseudo R^2 Nagelkerke value (.129), 1.2% of the variance in the response is attributed to the predictors in the model compared to the null model. Because a pseudo R^2 value of anything below .2 was considered a weaker result, one could approximate that the model may not have been the best fit (Shah, 2023). Therefore, the variance in the response variable was approximated by other extenuating variables beyond the predictor variables (Shah, 2023). The test of model effects found in Appendix B, Table 5 demonstrates statistically significant relationships with domestic violence ($p = .003$) and income ($p = < .001$). Considering the p-values, the test of model effects, and the pseudo R^2 values combined, it was determined that the variables were a moderately good fit for analysis of the model (Shah, 2023).

An increase in domestic violence never was associated with a decrease in days of mental health not good (OR = .613, 95% CI - .415 to .905). The p-value was .014 which was statistically significant. Resulting in a lower probability of women experiencing an increase in poor mental health days. In comparison, a woman experiencing domestic violence once (OR = .953, 95% CI - .514 to 1.77) in childhood was also associated with a decrease in mental health days not good. The p-value of .878 was not statistically significant.

A change in marital status was associated with a decrease in mental health days not good (OR = .501, 95% CI - .332 to .755). With a p-value of <.001, this result was statistically significant. As marital status changed to divorced, there was also an association with a decrease in mental health days not good (OR = .657, 95% CI - .406 to 1.06). The resulting p-value for this variable was .086, which was not statistically significant.

Full time employment was associated with a decrease in days mental health not good (OR = .529, 95% CI - .296 to .947). The p-value was .032, which was statistically significant. Self-employment was also associated with a decrease in mental health days not good (OR = .535, 95% CI - .264 to 1.08). However, as the work status changed to no work there was an interesting result. Investigating increases in employment status to that of homemaker demonstrated an association in increased mental health days not good (OR =

4.23, 95% *CI* - .279 to 64.08). The *p*-value for this result was .298. Being out of work for more than a year was associated with an increase in mental days not good (*OR* = 1.38, 95% *CI* - .498 to 3.84) with a *p*-value of .534 that was not statistically significant. For those out of work for less than one year, there was also an association with increased days mental health not good (*OR* = 1.51, 95% *CI* - .668 to 3.43). The *p*-value of .321 was not statistically significant. It was interesting to see that a lack of work was associated with an increase in days that mental health was poor for women. *Note.* Table 2 provides information from the ordinal regression related to the second research question investigating the relationships between the independent and dependent variables.

Table 2

Ordinal Regression Results for Marital Status, Employment, and Income

Parameter	B	t	p	Exp(B)	95% CI (Lower)	95% CI (Upper)
Days mental health not good (0- 9)	-.763	-2.41	.016	.466	.251	.868
Days mental health not good (10 -19)	-.077	-.234	.815	.926	.487	1.76
Days mental health not good (20 – 30)	.000			1.00		
		.	.	1.00	.	
DV Never	-.490	-2.46	.014	.613	.415	1.76

DV Once	-.048	-.153	.878	.953	.514	1.77
DV More than once	.000			1.00		
Married	-.691	-3.30	<.001	.501	.332	.755
Divorced	-.421	-1.72	.086	.657	.406	1.06
Separated	-.782	-2.44	.015	.457	.244	.858
Never married	-.000			1.00		
Employed full-time	-.636	-2.15	.032	.529	.296	.947
Self-employed	-.625	1.74	.082	.535	.264	1.08
Out of work >1year	.324	.622	.534	1.38	.498	3.84
Out of work <1 year	.414	.993	.321	1.51	.668	3.43
Homemaker	1.44	1.04	.298	4.23	.279	64.08
Student	-.494	.597	.407	.610	.189	1.97
Retired	.931	.283	.001	.394	.226	.687
Unable to work	.000			1.00		
Income	-.247	.063	<.001	.781	.691	.884

Dependent Variable: number of days mental health not good (Ascending)
Model: (Threshold), DV More than once, Never married, Unable
to work Link function: logit

Reviewing the correlation parameter estimates of the predictor and response variables allowed an inference that some changes in the response variable were not due to chance. Still, it represented an interaction among the variables (Salkind et al., 2020).

Therefore, the null hypothesis was rejected due to differences among the predictor and response variables from the sample (H_{2a}) and general (H_{20}) populations, which were explained by the above inferences, not chance alone.

Research Question 3

What is the relationship between mental health, sexual abuse, and substance use disorder in women with and without a history of domestic violence? H_{30}: There will be no relationship between mental health and sexual abuse and substance use disorder in women with a history of domestic violence.

H_{3a}: There will be a relationship between mental health and sexual abuse and substance use disorder in women with a history of domestic violence.

The ACEs analyzed to determine their appropriateness for inclusion in the model for substance use disorders were alcohol and drug misuse. The pseudo R^2 Nagelkerke value (.063) indicates that approximately 6.3% of the variation in the response was attributed to the predictors in the model compared to the null (Laerd Statistics, n.d.).

Investigating drinking at the level of no exposure in the home during childhood, there was an association with mental health days not good ($OR = 1.26$, 95% CI - .878 to 1.80). The p-value was .210, which was not statistically significant. .

Investigating drug use exposure during childhood at the level of no was associated with an increase in mental health days not good ($OR = 1.63$, 95% CI – 1.61 to 3.73) with a p-value of <.001 that was statistically significant. *Note.* Table 3 below provides the ordinal regression results for the independent variables for substance use disorder.

Note. Table 3 below provides the ordinal regression results for the independent variables for substance use disorder.

Table 3

Ordinal Regression Results for Drug and Alcohol Misuse

Parameter	B	t	p	Exp(B)	95% CI (Lower)	95% CI (Upper)
Days mental health not good (0- 9)	1.36	7.12	< .001	3.91	2.69	5.67
Days mental health not good (10 -19)	2.02 2.02	10.04	< .001	7.55	5.09	11.19
Days mental health not good (20 – 30)	.000			1.00		
		.	.	.		
DV Never	-.646	-3.30	<.001	.524	.357	.769
DV Once	-.105	.391	.696	1.11	.655	1.90
DV More than once	.000			1.00		
Drink no	.230	1.25	.210	1.26	.878	1.80
Drink yes	.000		.086	.657	.406	1.06
Drugs no	.896	4.16	<.001	1.63	1.61	3.73
Drugs yes	.000			1.00		

Dependent variable: Number of days mental health not good (Ascending)
Model: (threshold), DV more than once, Drink no, Drugs no
Link function: Logit

The ACEs analyzed to determine their appropriateness for inclusion in the model for sexual abuse were sexual abuse by being touched, by being made to touch someone else, and being forced to engage in sexual intercourse . The pseudo R^2 Nagelkerke value (.070) indicates that approximately 7.0% of the variation in the response was attributed to the predictors in the model compared to the null (Laerd Statistics, n.d.).

The independent variable sexual abuse by not being touched was associated with a decrease in days that mental health is poor (*OR* = .371, 95% *CI* - .116 to 1.19). The *p*value was .095, which was not statistically significant. As the variable sexual abuse for being touched exposure increased, there continued to be a decrease in mental days not good (*OR* =

.424, 95% *CI* - .104 to 1.72). The *p*-value was .231, which was not

statistically significant.

The independent variable sexual abuse by not being made to touch

someone was associated with an increase in mental health days not good (*OR*

= 5.07, 95% *CI* - .755 to 34.09) The *p*-value of .095 was not statistically

significant. As sexual abuse by being made to touch someone increased in

exposure to once, there was an increase in days that mental health was not

good (*OR* = 9.54, 95% *CI* – 1.17 to 77.64) The *p*-value of .035 was

statistically significant.

The independent variable for sexual abuse by not having sexual

intercourse with someone was associated with a decrease in mental health

days not good (*OR* = .103, 95% *CI* - .019 to .548). The *p*-value of .008 was

statistically significant. As incidents of being made to engage in sexual

intercourse with someone increased to once (*OR* = .294, 95% *CI* - .035 to

2.43), mental health days not good decreased. The *p*-value was .257, which

was not statistically significant. *Note.* Relationships among the variables are

better visualized using a relationship map, such as in Figure 16 below.

Figure 16

Relationships Among Substance Misuse, Domestic Violence, and Mental Health

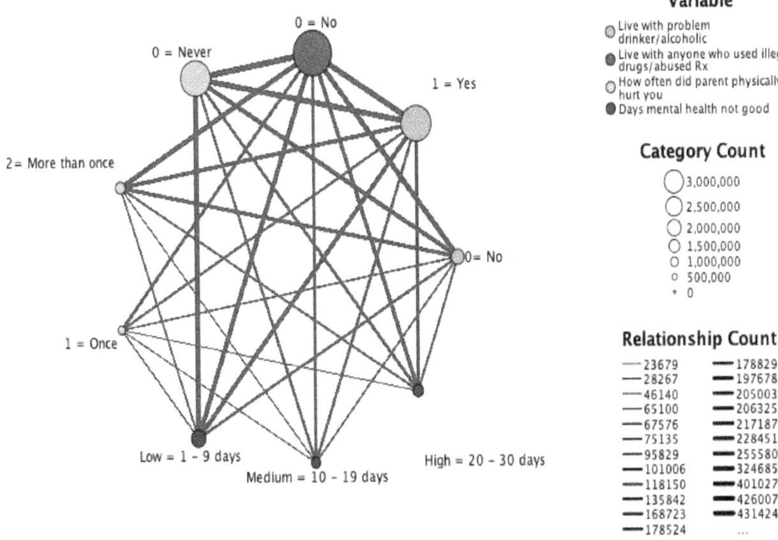

There was a higher number of women who reported exposure to domestic violence more than once during childhood in the home ($n = 1,000,000$) and who were exposed to drinking in the home ($n = 118,151$). The map also supports the results of the ordinal regression where women exposed to drinking in the home had a lower probability of increased days (low = 1-9 days) of poor mental health ($n = 178,829$). Considering the same factors for women who denied history of domestic violence and acknowledged exposure to drinking in the home ($n = 324,685$), the map displayed an increased number of women reporting lower days of mental health as not good ($n = 255,580$). Using the relationship map, various combinations were available for comparison and review. The variance in the response was not due to chance alone; therefore, one would reject the null hypothesis for substance use disorder (Salkind et al., 2020). Appendix C, Table 4 contains the complete ordinal regression for review.

Summary

With a thorough review of the predictor and response values, it was enlightening to see confirmation of the assumptions for some variables and not others. During the analysis, the scale data was not transformed to maintain the integrity of the continuous data format due to the weighting associated with those variables. All three research questions had impacts on the response variable. Whether the coefficient variables were negative or positive, the assumptions were met, the models of analyses were a good fit for the data, and the outcomes varied based on their unique contributions to the models for analysis. This in-depth investigation laid the foundation for the thoughtful application of the theoretical model to the analyses, planning for public health improvement, and disseminating the results. The next chapter will highlight discussions, conclusions, and recommendations.

Chapter 5: Discussion, Conclusions, and Recommendations

Introduction

This chapter concludes the study of the investigation into ACEs and

their relationship to the mental health of women with a history of domestic

violence. As this chapter progresses through each research question, it is

important to consider the relevance and contribution of the resulting analyses

to the field of knowledge. Although statistical significance is important to

show strong relationships and draw inferences in a study sample and the

general population, is not the only foundation for importance in research

(Mohajeri et al., 2020). It behooves researchers to consider the purpose of the

null hypothesis (H_o), which is the probability that the null is proven true

(Mohajeri et al.,

2020).

To discern the value of the null hypothesis, the *p*-value is the measure

of reference, such that any resulting *p*-value equivalent to or smaller than .05

indicates statistical significance, leading one to reject the null hypothesis

(Mohajeri et al., 2020). Some variables for the question with which they are

associated demonstrated statistical significance, while others did not. This

suggests that one should consider the real-world application of the variance in

the response and its lower and upper values (Mohajeri et al., 2020).

Each research question and the associated null and alternative

hypothesis will be discussed, along with the theoretical application to the study's premise and contributions to the public health community. This chapter will also review the limitations encountered and proposed opportunities for growth and development via future research endeavors.

Discussions

According to the South Carolina Coalition Against Domestic Violence and Sexual Assault (SCCADVASA, 2023), South Carolina ranks 11th for domestic violence against women. The latest statistic represents a slight improvement from ranking 12th as of 2022 (NCIPC, 2022). Updated statistics for 2023 show that 42.3% of women in South Carolina experience some form of domestic violence (SCCADVASA, 2023). According to earlier statistics, this is an unfortunate decrease, which indicated 41.5% in early 2023 (Domestic

Violence 2023, n.d.). According to The National Coalition Against Domestic Violence (n.d.), the national average of women impacted by domestic violence is 23.2%.

Compared to the national average, South Carolina has much room for improvement.

An ACE is a trauma experienced during childhood before age 18 (CDC et al..,

2021; Felitti, 2019). There are 10 ACEs in three categories: (a) *Child Mistreatment*

(physical, sexual, or emotional mistreatment), (b) *Neglect* (emotional and physical), and (c) *Household Dysfunction* (emotional malfunction, parent absenteeism due to incarceration, separation/divorce, substance use disorder, and physical violence against the mother) (Loxton et al., 2020; Ports et al., 2022). Witnessing one instance of an ACE or living through chronic ACE exposures during childhood has been documented to cause trauma affecting the developing brain, disruption of cognitive development, leads to adverse health outcomes in adulthood, and maladaptive social functioning (Fisher, 2019; Loxton et al., 2021; Ports et al., 2022).

I investigated the relationship between sexual abuse, household substance use disorder, marital status, employment, level of education, age, sex, and income, regarding their individual and combined influences on the mental health of women with a history of domestic violence in South Carolina. Further supporting the research proposal, the background and problem statement provided a basis for the study rationale. Reviewing the theoretical framework provided a foundation for public health policy development. Examining the literature review, methodology, analysis, and final discussion of the outcome, allowed for a well-rounded investigative discussion of the issue and possible mitigative efforts.

Discussion of Findings for Research Question 1 Analysis

What is the relationship between mental health and age, sex, and education of women with or without a history of domestic violence?

To investigate the relationship between mental health and age, sex, and education of women with or without a history of domestic violence, complex samples ordinal regression was conducted to analyze the variables. Results indicated that there was a change in the response or outcome variable. An 8.3% variance (Nagelkerke R^2 = .083) was detected in the response variable. There was statistical significance in education, age, and domestic violence (p = <.001) that support the Nagelkerke values. Women with a history of never having experienced domestic violence in childhood have a statistically lower probability of experiencing worsening mental health days that are not good. As the frequency of domestic violence exposure in childhood increased to at least once (OR = .945, 95% CI - .557 to 1.60), mental health days not good decreased, but was not statistically significant (p = .834). This result is aligned with current research in the field where increased exposure to domestic violence in the home yields decreased mental health malfunction (Lee et al., 2022).

Investigating the relationship between education and domestic violence with mental health days not good demonstrated a similar trend as that previously mentioned. As demonstrated in Figure 17, the higher the level of education, the lower the number of mental health days not good (Lee et al., 2022). A similar trend was discovered with age.

As age increased, the frequency of days that mental health was not good decreased (OR = .945, 95% CI - .557 to 1.60). Whether consideration of the variables was individual or cumulative for this question there was a significant impact on the response variable. Due to this change in the response variable, one would reject the null hypothesis.

Discussion of Findings for Research Question 2 Analysis

What is the relationship between mental health and marital status, income level, and employment in women with or without a history of domestic violence?

To investigate the relationship between mental health and marital status, income level, and employment in women with or without a history of domestic violence, complex samples ordinal regression was conducted to analyze the variables. With the variables considered for investigation for question two, multiple layers are involved with income, employment, and marital status, yielding hundreds of possible combinations. Investigating divorced (*OR* = .501, 95% *CI* - .332 to .755) or separated women (*OR* = .457, 95% *CI* - .244 to .858) with a history of domestic violence, I learned that the women experienced fewer days of mental health not good.

There was a significant association between income (*OR* = .781, 95% *CI* - .691 to .884) and mental health days not good, as the *p*-value = <.001. For every unit increase in income levels, days of mental health not good decreased. Due to the use of archival quantitative data, one cannot draw inferences from the data alone. It was demonstrated that as a homemaker (*OR* = 4.23, 95% *CI* - .279 to 64.08), there was a positive association with days of mental health not good. There is no earned income and less social interaction with external individuals or organizations. This could lead to increased depression or anxiety. Therefore, the null hypothesis was rejected (Salkind et al., 2020). What is unknown from the data analyzed is the specific nuances about employment status of no work that caused women to experience more days of poor mental health.

I anticipated that increased exposure to domestic violence in the home would be associated with increased days that mental health is poor. However, the opposite was demonstrated. Women experiencing increased childhood domestic violence in the home was associated with decreased days of poor mental health in adulthood (OR = .953, 95% CI - .514 to 1.77). Due to the influence of the predictor on the response variable, the null hypothesis was rejected (Salkind et al., 2020).

Discussion of Findings for Research Question 3 Analysis

What is the relationship between mental health, sexual abuse, and substance use disorder in women with and without a history of domestic violence?

To investigate the relationship between mental health, sexual abuse, and substance use disorder in women with or without a history of domestic violence, complex samples ordinal regression was conducted to analyze the variables. In keeping with recent studies, no alcohol misuse (OR = 1.26, 95% CI − .878 to 1.80) and no drug misuse (OR =

2.45, 95% *CI* – 1.61 to 3.73) were both associated with statistically

significant increases (p = <.001) in poor days of mental health (Lee et al.,

2022).

Women with a history of domestic violence once (*OR* = 1.11, 95% CI -

.655 to 1.89) demonstrated higher odds of experiencing increased days of

poor mental health compared to the null. A relationship map was provided in

Figure 6 to demonstrate the various relationships between the variables for

research question three. This was a strong set of relationships indicating that

the variance in the response variable was closely related to substance use

disorder, thus rejecting the null hypothesis.

Sexual abuse by the touch of someone else during childhood yielded

interesting outcomes. As exposure to sexual abuse by being touched

increased (*OR* = .371, 95% *CI* - .116 to 1.20), days of mental health not good

decreased. As the frequency of domestic violence increased to once (*OR* =

1.07, 95% *CI* - .620 to 1.83), days of mental health not good also increased.

There was also an interesting positive relationship between a woman being

made to touch someone as a form of sexual abuse. Touching someone once

(*OR* = 9.54, 95% *CI* – 1.17 to 77.64) was statistically significant in the

association with days of poor mental health. Like current research, ACEs

significantly impacted the response variable (Lee et al., 2022). The null

hypothesis was rejected due to the predictor association to the response

variable from the ACEs as predictors.

Reintroduction of the Problem Statement

I aimed to investigate how the mental health of women with a history of domestic violence may be impacted by age, sex, marital status, income, education, employment status, sexual abuse, and substance use disorder. The proposed premise was to provide women with the tools and services necessary to help them mitigate the effects of childhood trauma that can manifest in adulthood. The results of the study helped to identify areas of need. Although concerns were identified in the three questions, the selected focus for this project came from the final research question, focusing on women with a history of domestic violence and substance use disorder in the home. Based upon this discovery, services may be revised or developed to address ACEs about substance use disorder in the home experienced by children under 18.

Positive Social Change Impact

The positive social change impact from this research would have impactful outcomes for many children and benefit them in adulthood. It is understood from previous research that ACEs are related to increased chronic health issues such as mental health concerns (depression, stress, emotional problems), Type II diabetes, increased cardiovascular risks, and other chronic health complications (Bouwens et al., 2023; Loxton et al., 2021). From the findings discussed, it was revealed that substance use disorder was statistically significant in its impact on the mental health of women with a history of domestic violence.

The results from this research aligned with current research studies, including substance use disorder (Bouwens et al., 2023; Loxton et al., 2021). Emphasis should be placed on services provided to women undergoing treatment for substance use disorder with children in the home to mitigate the future of those children replicating what they have witnessed (Bouwens et al., 2023; Loxton et al., 2021). Completing ACEs assessments with the women in treatment and evolving their treatment to include targeted psychotherapy inclusive of the children harmed would impact the children before adulthood.

Theoretical Application of the Social Ecological Model

Interpersonal and Intrapersonal Level of SEM

Theoretical consideration of the findings within the SEM would encourage one to consider environmental alterations rather than focus on the individual (Bronfenbrenner, Hayden, 2019). Age, sex, and education are identified at the microsystem level, where interpersonal relationships are formed. This includes relationships with parents, siblings, other relatives, and friends at school and in the local community. Relationships at the innermost level of the model are shaped by experiences impacting individual values, perception, knowledge, and personality development (Hayden, 2019). Developing trusting relationships at this level of the model is crucial to a child being trusting enough to report domestic violence, sexual abuse, or other concerns in the home environment or elsewhere. Working from the environmental perspective with substance use may warrant more creative provision of services such as revising services that women already receive. Those services should be co-located rather than sending the woman to another facility for therapy. Understanding how behavior is influenced by what is modeled by friends, family, or even classmates helps one understand how at the interpersonal and intrapersonal levels in the SEM, careful placement of services in the environment for access by those who influence behavior is pivotal (Hayden, 2019). The South Carolina Department of Mental Health could designate therapists for addiction treatment facilities specializing in trauma or ACE assessment combined with addiction therapeutic services.

Community Level of SEM

Considering marital status, income, and employment at the macrosystem level is more reflective of community services one may encounter for support. This may include reviewing policies and procedures impacting those receiving or providing services (Hayden, 2019). Employment may include incentive programs for abstaining from risky health behaviors. Regarding children, it may include more aggressive programs regarding vaping, smoking, drug use, and bullying (Hayden, 2019). Because this research, along with other current studies (Bouwens et al., 2023), aids in understanding that adults with a history of substance use disorder are twice as likely to develop future drug dependence, it is imperative to have behavioral and physical health care providers specifically trained in better understanding ACEs and their role in developing children and adolescents. It is also important to have this training when working with adults to understand the current impact from past trauma (Felitti, 2019; Felitti et al., 2019; Fisher, 2019).

We also know that influence at this level of intervention can be beneficial coming from persons trusted to those seeking assistance. Local church involvement with community health partners providing ancillary services can benefit many in a nontraditional manner. Others may find solace in school guidance counselors or communitybased events that are provided in connection with local schools. Therapeutic interventions offered through employee assistance programs (EAP) may also lessen the stigma often associated with more traditional forms of seeking help. With the availability of telehealth, it is possible to receive assistance in more private settings than in years past.

Societal Level of SEM

The chronosystem level of intervention focuses on substance use disorder, domestic violence, and sexual abuse. The ACEs identified here are the most frowned upon by society (Hayden, 2019). Therefore, admitting to being a victim or a perpetrator of any of these acts can elicit strong reactions from society. There are societal rules and regulations for dispensing prescription medications, smoking, and alcohol intake. These rules govern one's behavior based on adherence to these rules or lack thereof (Hayden, 2019). Therefore, should one partake of illegal drugs, abuse prescription medications, or be charged with driving under the influence (DUI), there can be an arrest and judgment by one's peers in a court of law. Therefore, a health professional may encounter high recidivism rates in the client population with whom they work as the client ebbs and flows between all the levels in the SEM. There may be judgment or rejection from family and friends that prompts someone with a history of trauma to abuse drugs or alcohol to cope with the pain from the past (Fisher, 2019). Indulging in substance misuse may result in them being caught up in the legal system, losing their children, being mandated to drug and alcohol counseling, losing employment, housing, income, etc. It is for that reason that the SEM is the most appropriate model from which to approach proactive and creative behavior change from the individual, community, and societal considerations (Bouwens et al., 2023; Felitti et al, 2019; Fisher, 2019; Hayden, 2019).

Recommendations

Based on the review of the SEM from the analytical perspective of the research questions, my recommendation remains to focus on substance use disorder and its propensity to predict adverse mental health outcomes in women with a history of domestic violence. Conducting ACEs assessments on women meeting those criteria would be most effective. Targeting services to that specific population would be more cost-effective and has the potential for the highest return on investment over time.

For successful implementation of the recommendations, the research and the results must be disseminated to the leaders in the field who can seriously consider funding and effecting policy change at the local and state levels. Budgets must be amended, requested, and allocated. These actions take place at the state legislature level, which takes time. For those receiving the services, there should be a discussion with them in a confidential manner to get their feedback on the planned services and whether they would consider them beneficial. Focus groups would be fruitful as you can receive anecdotal information unavailable in archival data analysis. Services could be tailored from the data analysis with the qualitative responses to formulate the most efficacious program to meet the needs of this population.

Future Implications

Continued study is recommended to consider other independent variables that may have an undetermined relationship to mental health. Questions of consideration for future inquiry may include investigating a relationship between the mental health of incarcerated women with a history of domestic violence and (a) marital status, income, and employment; (b) age, sex, and education level; and (c) sexual abuse, recidivism, and substance use. It may also be beneficial to consider a mixed methods study where some anecdotal information may be considered to better the phenomena of the increase in age being related to a decrease in poor mental health outcomes (Lee et al., 2022).

Summary

ACEs have been studied beginning around 1998 by Felitti and continue to be important in understanding the behaviors of adults today. Children worldwide encounter various issues in the home, from witnessing their mothers injured during domestic violence attacks to being victims of sexual or physical abuse themselves (Bouwens et al., 2023; Fisher, 2019; Felitti, 2019). As health professionals continue to assist women with overcoming their daunting circumstances, there continues to be something derailing their success. It's learned behavior. During the formative years of development, traumas experienced in the home could be indelibly etched into one's mind and could unconsciously predetermine future direction (Fisher, 2019). Unknowingly one would have learned from interactions with friends, family, and close associates in their community, that such behaviors were normal and even expected in life. Through research such as this and others in the world, women are learning that they can change their futures to be something other than what they may have been taught. They have come to understand that through better management of their mental health concerns (depression, stress, emotional problems) via therapy, they can control their future and that of their children. These women have developed a resilience that has carried them into success.

This is the positive imprint I want to leave through this research project; working with local leaders to make a difference in women's and children's lives for years to come.

This analysis delineated the concerns with substance use disorder related to the mental health difficulties of women with a history of domestic violence. The results reported aligned with current studies conducted in other parts of the world (Bouwens et al., 2023). I hope to further this initial research endeavor to include other variables to deepen the investigative review of the mental health of women with a history of domestic violence.

Conclusion

There was a television program discussing issues hindering the success of female victims of domestic violence as they leave an abusive relationship to create a safer life for themselves and their children. It was an enlightening discussion with women who survived domestic violence and interacted with community-based programs to help them continue to recover and regain their strength and independence. They discussed the role models they had and their resiliency tactics. As I began investigating potential topics of interest to me as a researcher, I wondered what may have influenced young girls and may have encouraged them to select a different trajectory. I learned about ACEs and how they contributed to generational behaviors. There were also environmental and societal factors that impacted outcomes as adults (Dube, 2022).

It then became apparent that there may be a need to investigate ACEs and the environmental and societal influences that had impacted the mental health of women with a history of domestic violence in South Carolina and how that may be addressed during childhood development. This is what changed my thoughts about a research topic. Because the issue of domestic violence is multifaceted, I decided to focus on the potential root causes. Thus, the investigation into the influence of ACEs, environmental, and societal factors on the mental health of women with a history of domestic violence. Investigating archival data of women's childhood history related to violence provided an opportunity to predict mental health outcomes in women exposed to specific ACEs while considering other independent variables.

An investigation into the relationship between ACEs and the mental health of women with a history of domestic violence was informative. It revealed that assumptions initially made were not as strong in predicting the mental health difficulties of women with mental health as did others. It revealed that more work is needed on a local and state level to secure funding and personnel to address the issue more adequately. It also revealed that although much work is yet to be done, it can be successful.